Navigating the Rivers of Cash

A leadership and strategy book to arm ambitious business leaders with inspiration and ideas to accelerate growth, shareholder value and wealth, whilst creating a sustainable purpose in society.

Kevin Uphill

Thorogood Publishing Ltd

10-12 Rivington Street
London EC2A 3DU
Telephone: 020 7749 4748

Email: info@thorogoodpublishing.co.uk
Web: www.thorogoodpublishing.co.uk

A CIP catalogue record for this book is available
from the British Library.

Paperback ISBN: (10) 1854188682
(13) 9781854188687

Ebook ISBN: (10) 1854188690
(13) 9781854188694

Printed and bound in Great Britain
by Marston Book Services Limited,
Oxfordshire

Table of Contents

About the author

Kevin Uphill has enjoyed a long and successful career as an entrepreneur, strategist and mergers and acquisitions advisor. Having successfully owned and sold several companies, he has in-depth business expertise. He is currently founder and Chairman of Avondale Group (www.avondale.co.uk), a leading international M&A boutique founded in 1991. The practice also has a Business Mentoring and Strategy division specialising in enhancing shareholder value.

In addition, Kevin is a respected speaker and leader on business strategy and journeys, mergers and acquisitions. He enjoys helping individuals and organisations realise their aspirations by sharing his knowledge and experience via mentoring, speaking and writing (www.mandamentor.co.uk). He is also the author of *How to Buy and Sell a Business for Wealth* and there is another book due in 2016; please ask for details.

Kevin is married with two children (the best in the world). He is a keen skier, triathlete, charity contributor, and property restorer. He is probably an intellectual, although he is still pondering the definition, so he may simply be compensating for doing badly at school.

About the book

This is a practical business book in which the author seeks to inspire business leaders to create and build exceptional businesses with a sustainable purpose in society whilst themselves becoming more insightful, strategic, creative and purposeful. The author shares simple ideas, outlooks and questions with the aim for the reader to draw conclusions that are unique to their personality, environment and objectives – thus navigating more effective journeys and achieving better understanding and outstanding results.

Introduction

Navigating the Rivers of Cash *is a leadership and strategy book to arm ambitious business leaders with inspiration, to accelerate growth, shareholder value and wealth whilst creating a sustainable purpose in society.*

It is very easy to be complacent about business as you get more confident, successful or higher up the ladder; but why is it some people seem to find the right direction more easily, and achieve far better results more quickly whilst still enjoying the journey? Conversely, why do some people eventually get ground down, plateau or decline? At its simplest level, success lies in leaders employing the right strategy with the right people, in the right way, in alignment. This is effectively the 'what' to do. However, of equal importance to tangible and valuable results, yet less analysed, is the 'how' and specifically the influence of the leader's outlook. That is, the business leader's ability to listen to, understand, and feel the strategic direction of a business in a positive, clear, energetic and ambitious way. How can business leaders through their own 'outlook' and insight personally influence commitment, accelerate growth, purposefulness, profits and shareholder value.

My explorations are not an instructional self-improvement book because, as a business leader or entrepreneur, you hate being told what to do. You are what you are, and are already well informed; also successful leadership does not come from information but from understanding. Understanding both of yourself and of other people creates the ability to motivate, influence and persuade people to move from one idea or place to another. An instruction book would be consultancy, and you know your business and your true strengths, weaknesses and resourcefulness far better than any consultant. My experience with clients has taught me that a successful prescription in one case would just as likely be a spectacular disaster in another. So, as opposed to advice that typically sits 'persuading' itself on the shelf, I hope good questions will instead influence and create resonance in new horizons and new ideas. Questions save us both from moralising parables and case studies; besides there is no certainty or set way, so why seek it with set advice?

My title is inspired by the idea of achieving better business flow through increasing clarity in the outlook of leaders. Flow is the 'enjoyable' state where the business activities are fully engaged, involved and effective. Flow can be achieved with clear naviga - tion by business leaders, who have understanding and whose emotions are channelled, positive and aligned with the task at hand.

The metaphor of the river is inspired by Herman Hesse's novel *Siddartha*, whose eponymous hero ends up as a river boat man. Hesse's story shares the idea that enlightenment is not attained through intellectual methods, nor through immersing oneself in the carnal pleasures of the world. Instead, that it is the completeness and richness of these experiences that create understanding. The idea here is that as business leaders we only achieve enlightenment if we experiment, if we learn and listen, which all adds to achieving a positive outlook. Every action or event leads to understanding, and it is the richness of this learning process that drives success. In this book, the carnal pleasure is the selfish pursuit of money, Wall Street style.

If money is the only driver, then we end up with short-term selfish decision making, reduced sustainability and a failure to align with customers, market trends or our teams.

The river in the title is the global market, and it flows very quickly; therefore, as leaders we must listen and feel it, rather than exhaust ourselves fighting it. In the river metaphor there is also the idea that everything is interlinked and continuous; rivers flow to oceans which turn to rain and replenish rivers. So it is with markets; they are interlinked, cyclical and continuous. Rivers can also only flow forward and so it is with decisions. Past decisions have been made, they either worked or didn't; but as leaders we must look objectively forward to what are the right decisions today to take advantage of the flow and the market's direction. I hope the metaphor will bring a visualisa- tion that helps you to navigate further ahead and stay more focused, with a greater freshness, sense of adventure, energy and clarity.

- *Are you and your team learning and changing faster than the market is flowing?*

- *What 'feel' do you have for the market and how far ahead do you navigate in it?*

A key component to the book is the idea that business leaders spend far too much time 'managing' day-to-day problems which they don't enjoy, instead of leading the business to growth and success, which they do enjoy. I examine why this happens and how to create shifts in the leader's time to encourage greater dedication to research, resolving challenges (not problems) at source, and navigating ahead more effectively with clarity, confidence, and energy. "Is Fred any good at his job?" is a management question. "Where is the market going, and how can we as an organisation catch the 'flow' more effect-ively and with purposefulness?" is a leadership question.

- *How much time do you spend managing as opposed to leading?*

In this question I effectively ask what the role and the 'outlook' of the Managing Director and the CEO in an organisation should be, in order to increase their effectiveness. To answer this we usually need to start with a firm look at our own personal approach and habits, as well as the second-tier talent in the team and how much they contribute to driving business growth and evolution rather than maintaining the status quo. As rivers only flow forward, I suggest we need to 'get over' our past, which reduces agility and stifles growth, and redesign our businesses by looking ahead further. Essentially how can leaders look at strategy and business design anew, so that they increase objectivity and remove preconceptions, in order to innovate and drive positive change? How can they achieve this whilst increasing both profit and shareholder value?

- *How well designed is your business?*

- *How much are preconceptions holding you and your team back?*

- *How do you grow profits and shareholder value?*

Whilst I have posed the questions with – primarily – the profes-sionally employed or self-made CEO reader in mind, I also seek to address senior managers, entrepreneurs and the ambitious. There are a lot of excellent textbooks, business models, organ-isational theory and toolkits for the role of the CEO already, so instead of replication I have attempted to navigate a different course and examine more the outlook, mindset and time-focus that might help to create better organisations and more valuable results. I believe the normal, or traditional textbook role of the CEO is that it is their responsibility to run the board and liaise with stakeholders whilst leading, setting and overseeing the implementation of the company's long and short-term plans. To achieve this they must also ensure the right personnel, organisational structure and appropriate costs relative to the strategy and opportunity; whilst in the process they must manage risks, systems, checks and controls, maintaining high standards throughout... Exhausted yet? I am, and that's why I think understanding the outlook is as critical as describing and being good at the role.

In addressing the potential outlook of business leaders in the river analogy, I hope also to inspire leaders to be more natural, forward flowing and fresh. By looking ahead at the course in front, not worrying about the past, and by listening to the river market more carefully, we gain higher understanding. We can then feel the market's flow and navigate a better course by setting clear waymarks and by building high quality adventurer teams who can share our explorations.

Often in the 'city' (the business) we become overstressed; the noise, the bustle, the concrete becomes too much and we can't hear ourselves think. Don't get me wrong, I love the city, but to be more successful – I believe – as business leaders, we have a responsibility to try and connect with nature - that is ours and our business's nature - more effectively. I explore the idea that business leaders are often overstressed and missing the contemplation that would increase their natural resourceful - ness. I contend that too often we keep busy as opposed to smart, with long unproductive hours and bustle for the sake of it. This immersion can reduce our ability to add purposefulness to both our lives and our businesses and the bustle and compet - iveness can make us selfish. A great business is much more than just about making money. Of course this must be a func-tion, but can we also make a difference to society, our fellow workers and thus increase purposefulness? Can we design and build more successful, natural, sustainable and purposeful busi-nesses and how do we do that? I suggest that businesses which make a difference grow more quickly, they engage and retain better talent and increase client/market demand which drives growth. As I write on my computer, the vision of a PC on every person's desk in the world has long driven growth in that sector, but in what way does it 'make a difference'? For the first time it democratises human knowledge and that is the real reason the story has been so successful. What is the purpose behind your business design, product and service?

- *How do you and your business make a difference?*

The US Declaration of Independence sets out the human right to "Life, liberty, and the pursuit of happiness". Today, America's richest 400 people have more financial wealth than the bottom 100 million people collectively, and there is almost no social mobility. Advancement has stalled both in belief and access – is this Capitalism's legacy? In the 18th and 19th centuries, Western civilisation was exponentially spurred on by avid self-improvers and adventurers, who believed it was right to be successful but who were also looking at their contribution to society; people like John Cadbury or Andrew Carnegie, who built fortunes but who also looked at what wealth might do for humanity. Andrew Carnegie famously quoted, "You can't help the poor unless you are rich." In other words, the pursuit of wealth is critical in a money-based economy, but at the same time there should be some determination to give something back. Further, we don't all have the wealth to be philanthropic, but as leaders we need to ask, "What do our businesses day-to-day contribute to humanity in a wider sense and why?" If we

can answer this question, it gives clearer direction to the business, which in itself increases the growth, the flow and the
sense of purpose. I also suggest that acting to serve 'all' as
opposed to just oneself increases the ability to lead, and
enhances individual happiness.

The river, as well as being the market, is also 'pure and natural'
– seeking to align capitalism and business growth with making
a difference to humanity and sustainability. Of course this is a
big idea, but my point is on a strategic basis; even if every business leader asked the question and acted differently in only a
small way, we would continue in the zeitgeist of the current
times to dramatically improve the world. I am an optimist in
this respect; I believe the current times have already made
enormous leaps in improving education, in access to freedom
and knowledge, with fewer wars, less famine and disease and
an increase in the individual and collective moral conscious-
ness; but I also believe we can achieve far more if we continue
the conversation. The question "How do you and your business
contribute?" is designed to help you increase growth as well as
make a difference. The best companies are the ones where
leaders produce valuable results but also feel good about the
people they work with and their organisations.

- *How clear is your direction; not only 'what' to do, but most
  importantly 'why'?*

- *What changes need to be made?*

Albert Einstein defined insanity as doing the same thing over
and over again and expecting different results, yet in many
businesses this is what occurs. Broadly, the business model is
built on a layer cake of history; the plan is often entirely incremental, with such small changes that the result is the status quo
is maintained, at best. Growth requires leadership, changing

habits, intelligence, understanding and purpose, not necessarily hard work. Think of your car: the one you own today is a lot better than the one you had 20 years ago; it's much faster, more reliable, quiet and ergonomic. These changes happened because time and resources had been invested in design to purpose – not by chance.

- *How much time have you spent designing the purpose of your business?*

- *How and where can you find this time?*

Finally, in the 'navigation' concept, I examine the role of the leader in future thinking and goal setting. The river is choppy and there are lots of rapids. It's tiring, particularly if the wrong course or direction is maintained and, as leaders, we have a responsibility to take the time to look ahead objectively. Of course, if we could predict or navigate the future with absolute certainty then business would be easy, but the winners are the leaders who more often set (or appear to set) the right course, at the right time. Therefore, looking ahead and setting a clearer course with readily identifiable and mapped waymarks that everyone understands is a vital function of 'getting it right' and creating better results. However, we also need to understand that markets today change rapidly and it is important to avoid over-rigid navigation; the ability to make fast changes and to adapt in direction and adjustment are skills that are just as necessary and vital as the ability to be right. Whilst I suggest we need to increase our awareness of strategic options, in today's churning global market we also need to find techniques and methods to create rapid change and evolution in our busi - nesses.

In summary, I have set out to present new ideas and questions that will help you to look at your business leadership outlook, habits and focus – as well as your strategy – with refreshed innovation and perspective. I also aim to help you guide and navigate with more effective strategy in order to increase purposefulness, business growth and shareholder value. In this book I ask you to join me on a journey, exploration and adven - ture.

Chapter 1
Navigating by design

Introduction

As an ambitious leader you are willing to do what it takes to create more purposeful businesses that accelerate growth, profits and shareholder value. In this chapter I seek questions to explore how leaders can achieve this strategically by shifting their time, attention and habits. What can they do to break free of predetermination and distraction and secure a more creative outlook that will help set and navigate a simpler and more effective course in the river?

It is the role of the business leader to navigate a successful course for business growth, profits, purpose and shareholder value. They are also responsible for overseeing its implementa - tion and evolution, yet too often they can be trapped in the web of history or caught in management rather than leadership. By that I mean caught in legacy, the path the business has taken by design, accident, market force or inertia and managing 'hands on' rather than designing and leading improvement, 'hands off'. The strategy many leaders often employ is a pile strategy – over-layering new strategy on the old. I call this 'layer cake' because it is fattening! This generally creates incremental growth at best and, at worst, can result in decline as a result of inefficiency with too many elements poorly performing, worn-out or tugging in different directions and adversely affecting figures and increasing the need for constant management resource. Yet studies and my experience show that fast-track businesses are achieved when leaders quietly analyse their businesses from the ground up, and design intelligently with no great adherence to history. In this they move from management to leadership, they design a business based on the likely future trends rather than tradition, and objectively allow no predeter - mination in creating fresh perspectives.

Today talent, that is being good at the job, is just an invite to the party and it can be enough if you want to create a 'reasonable' business, but an 'exceptional' business also requires crafted design – creating and designing the right platform (the processes, goals and direction) for that talent to be leveraged efficiently and effectively. Combining this with satisfying customers' needs and ensuring margin capitalises on the river's flow (the market) in the right way.

Overall, therefore, leaders need to take the time and care to strategically navigate and set the right course; a talented long-distance runner will be beaten to the finishing line by a walker over 25 miles if they are just two degrees off course.

Michael Gerber, in his famous book E-Myth, explores the idea that business owners are held back by working in and not on the business; further, that it is the curse of the entrepreneur being good at a trade which allows them to work in the busi - ness. The mantra instead is we should work on our businesses, think of the business as a franchise. In other words, build a business with repeatable and scalable processes that can be easily replicated. This is excellent advice and will increase shareholder value as it reduces the business's dependency on the leadership, increasing scalability and sustainability. In addi - tion, because of the simplicity employed, it ensures the model can be duplicated. However in the 'lead' as opposed to 'manage' thesis we go beyond just good processes when working 'hands on' in the business. Instead we move 'hands off' into the creative and research space, leading the business into the future-thinking arena rather than managing current trends and incremental change.

In the river concept, a better design will make things flow more easily, increase ergonomics and purposefulness. Too often, business leaders knee jerk to current circumstance – 'managing' businesses day-to-day with poor underlying incremental strategy rather than 'leading' with intelligent long-term goals and direction. As a result, they end up fighting the river (market) only to create dissatisfying, stressful and exhausting short-term wins requiring constant effort and long hours. With the right navigation, can we design and lead purposeful busi - nesses where our customers and teams engage by influence and drive growth by reputation rather than persuasion, with values and a culture that make a difference? Imagine a carefully 'designed' map which shows, in a series of pictures, the ulti - mate direction with waymarks (goals) along the way. The map defines the specifications, strategy, model, infrastructure, para - meters, costs, activities, and processes against the opportunity. It sets out how and what to do within environmental constraints in order to achieve that direction and opportunity.

- *If you had a blank script how would you choose to design your business afresh?*

Overall I contend that more successful businesses are created when leaders take the time and energy to research, design and then drive change with fresh perspectives. However, the river flows quickly today so that 'design' is now an evolutionary constant. Globalisation, digital communication and knowledge access now mean that markets move very quickly. If we accept this, we therefore need to find faster, simpler ways than tradi -

tional top-down, management-set strategy, which we simply don't have the time for and will always follow the market rather than lead the market. I therefore believe that, today, a team-driven model with the 'leadership' assessing the overall direc - tion and waymarks and the team 'managing' and working out each specific with an adaptive approach is critical. Further, I have been careful to talk about design to direction as opposed to destinations. Fluid markets have a tendency to shift destina - tions and arriving actually creates pinnacles. Business, change and opportunity are a constant, so a clearly navigated direction rather than destination is usually more effective.

If a fast market current is a constant there are many options and opportunities – but how do we decide on the course? By designing a business that allows leaders to take time to muse, to ask questions and think about how to set an intelligent course. If you combine ample strategic free time with future thinking, research and great analytics on customer servicing trends, it becomes quite clear which design and course is right. Uncer - tainty is usually caused by a lack of strategic free time, a lack of research and development of trends data or   failure to analyse past inefficiencies.

- *How much research time do you have to dedicate to analytics?*

By taking the time to research and design a business model and system where the team and market create the drive, the pres - sure is taken off the leader so they have strategic free time. Strategic free time is not effortless; it requires significant input in research, listening, analysis and change management, ensuring the design and course is clear, confident and in purpose. It means confidently ignoring the negative pressures that we face daily and instead concentrating on the things we care about beyond ourselves and self-interest; disciplined, flex ible and with a sense of purpose to stay the course despite the many counter currents. Great business leaders charismatically lead the change via patient passion, clear intelligent strategy and absolute unswerving belief that there is a way to make a difference, and a reason to make a difference and be the best.

- *How much time do you spend on leading the business – setting the direction and waymarks – as opposed to managing the business?*

- *How team driven is your management?*

As in the example we looked at earlier, your car is better today by far than the one you had 20 years ago. This happened as a result of extraordinary amounts of research, development and competitive analysis. With hybrid and electric (and possibly hydrogen?), the future is radically different and this is happening by research, design, creativity, investment, change and imagination, which manufacturers are forced to employ to compete and protect the environment. Every business leader has in reality the same responsibility, yet if you ask how much time most business leaders spend on navigating ahead with 'hands off' rather than 'hands on', the answer is nearly always disproportionally in the managing space. This might explain why there are so few fast-track great companies: quite simply because the leaders are either too incremental in the changes they implement, too cautious in their decisions, or too 'hands on' to take the time to design. A great example of short-termism was when IBM, despite at the time working with Bill Gates to create MSDos, 'perhaps' because they thought hardware was the future, then allowed Bill to wholly keep the licensing in 1981, ergo Microsoft.

Almost every sector has a David and Goliath story, where small beats large; why is that? Case studies identify the nimbleness of the Davids, the smaller companies, but actually how much of this is because the small companies are younger, more agile and sometimes more naïve? This agility and fresh perspective enables them to seek instinctively and to anticipate the future market as opposed to seeking to dominate the current one. Perhaps ultimately this is because the smaller companies (the Davids) radically just never understood the rules of the current market and are not beholden to the limited thinking this breeds.

Further, many business leaders are too close to their business or industry, which means they tend to think 'specifics' when it comes to their strategy, but 'specifics' can make us beholden to history and the fattening strategy 'layer cake'. Being initially too caught in the specifics or the 'how' can be inhibiting or disabling and can result in a negative outlook, leaving us ignoring the big picture and future trends. The conversation falls into, "We can't own that space because our competitors do" or, "We tried that and it didn't work; yet maybe the timing or implementation was wrong, not the idea?" Or, "We don't have the financial muscle, our team are not quite right for that." It's almost a form of creationism, an assumption by leaders that where the business is now is best explained by intelligent cause, and this is 'right' due to the complexity of the design, yet complexity is born of evolution which is a continuous process, always favouring those most adaptable to the environment.

A Business by Design strategy can guide you to achieve 'next-level growth' but it may require you and the business to face a period of disruption, fear and uncertainty before comfort is secured. These feelings can very heavily influence decisions, but business moves in cycles and usually the right direction with the market or ahead of the market will quickly result in comfort.

It is important that we become used to these cycles and actually embrace them rather than avoid them, because as soon as you secure comfort it probably means the next level is in reach and you need to look at significant further change. In this respect as leaders we learn to go with the flow (see Chapter 3) as opposed to fear, worry and overexertion to help us with uncertainty. As well as periods of discomfort, business design may also require consolidation before you can go forward to create secure foundations. Growth sought and over layered on poor design and foundations is at best slow and usually painful. Expansion against the right model is much less risky, but many leaders are so competitive that they only envisage 'forward' as progress, against all logic. I have never won a game of chess without sacrificing a piece or having to play defensive moves.

- *How can we help our customers more profitably?*

Design initiatives may also involve a temporary backwards strategy in terms of products or client types in order to create a clear stand-out position. This is known as the 'lose in order to gain' principle. Most businesses that fast track down the river get in a narrow current which is highly efficient and it drives them along. By this I mean they get known for being particu - larly good at something and customers start to seek them out, as opposed to their always having to seek new clients, which is hard work. Further, they have the intelligence and design to ensure they choose the right customers. The company knows the type of customers it wants (the high margin/least demanding) and does not worry when it chooses to say no to the other type. Indeed setting up your sales focus so that you can get to 'no' quickly is a critical part of design. Imagine you are a service business, and the customer you meet just does not understand the added value aspect, and is always looking for the lowest cost whilst still expecting you to maintain service levels. That is the customer to say no to. Being clear which customers you don't want enables you to concentrate on finding the ones you do want. Retailers are actually really good at this. Have you ever walked into an outfitters and got the feeling you don't belong there, either too cheap or too expensive? This is the 'lose in order to gain' principle. Most retailers know who they want as customers and set out their stall accordingly. They rarely seek to appeal to all as they know the niche that works for them; trying to have mass appeal in fashion is almost impossible.

- *How and where do you need to lose in order to gain?*

- *How do you align services and products ahead so that the market drives demand?*

Leadership not management

In the By Design concept, I have contended that leaders are often over-focused on management, stifling intelligent design and creativity, but why does this happen? Typically this is due to a mixed recipe – the ingredients being poor delegation, lack of clarity in job roles, ineffective second-tier talent and the leader - ship not giving themselves permission to take creative time out. An amusing metaphor with a moral is the one where a group of people are standing by a river. They hear a baby crying and rush to the riverbank to see a baby floating past, half drowned. One of the group immediately dives in to rescue the child. However, yet another baby comes floating down the river, and then another! Yet again, one of the group jumps in to save each baby. The group then see that the one person still on shore has started to walk away. Shocked, the group cry: "Where are you going?" The response? "I am going upstream to stop whoever is throwing these babies into the river." Being a leader requires you to step back, look at things differently, and not be afraid to stand out and to tackle problems at their cause or source. Management will always steal time for leadership as it has a louder voice and is more obvious, and therefore on the surface more comfortable, but it rarely grows exceptional companies.

In respect of delegation and second-tier talent, this takes careful investment in recruitment, training resource and the right remuneration combined with clarity and accountability. Do your team ask you questions and bring problems that are actu - ally within their remit? Are you answering questions they should or do know the answer to? Rather than telling people the answer, developing a quality second tier requires the lead - ership to shift to a coaching mindset as opposed to consulting. That is, instead of giving the answer, asking more often for the team to examine the question and generate the solution. This might be slower initially but ultimately increases second-tier initiative and quality dramatically.

Many businesses have been designed but more often, particu - larly in the small and mid-tier (less than 100 staff), they were started by someone good at a job with the ambition to make a lot of money. Because they were good at that job and still are good at that job, the business has grown and become quite successful, but at some point in my experience many of those businesses plateau, or hit void. That is they stop growing at the pace they were and occasionally even decline or fail. This is often because the entrepreneur who is good at innovation and deal making or the job/profession is rarely also good at processes and management. However, once a business gets to a certain size, management becomes more important. By their very nature, entrepreneurs are usually mavericks so all these words fill them with dread and instead they rant, "Why can't my team be more like me? Why are they not as motivated?" The simple answer for these entrepreneurs is that most people do not have the right skills or motivations. Many people do not have the risk appetite (even more so in Britain than say the US or China) or the ambition to drive business growth. Their ambition is family time, and metaphorically coaching the Sunday football team; they just are not that capitalistic or enterprising . That means a business can never wholly rely on employee self-motivation and instead needs to rely on tracking, clarity and responsibility.

As with species evolution (Darwin), it is not the strongest or most intelligent companies that survive, it is the ones that are the most adaptable to change. Too often, business owners focus on strength, maintaining market position incrementally rather than 'change', adapting fast to survive. An adaptive and flexible culture in fast-moving markets actually needs to be designed into the business. The core team need to have the free rein to 'give it a go', try and fail, not just to manage the status quo. There is always a much better way for you and your team, you just have to find it.

- *How adaptable and agile are you?*

Navigating further ahead

Business leaders who better anticipate future trends and innovation – and align the business around these – succeed more often, but markets are now moving faster, and they are also increasingly complex. Research is therefore absolutely critical; however, it is often assumed to only be relevant in technical environments yet, what your customers, suppliers and competition are or will be thinking is or becomes the market's flow.

Sustainable companies are not being built by chance, they 'get over' their history, look ahead and down the river, anticipating the white water, the ebbs and flows. Interestingly, further studies show that the biggest strategic initiatives rarely bear fruit with 24 months so short-term profit needs actually under - mine anticipation.

The strategy is to design a business that identifies new territ - ories, products, alliances, models and infrastructures that enhance flexibility and scalability; a design that comes from historic analysis combined with future thinking and has lots of inputs rather than ideals. There is a danger in the leadership concept that the balance of work ends up in the thought space but once analysis has been carried out and the course set, it is vital as usual to initiate detailed and specific action plans.

- *How do we widen our thinking?*

Think like an investor

Redesign also involves financial investment and risk. In this respect, I urge business leaders to think like an investor when investing in design and strategic change to grow a business. Investment in growth is usually tax deductible, yet capital on sale in most regimes is usually highly tax efficient. Building up a company for sale is a highly tax efficient method of creating wealth, but 'investments' need to generate a Return on Invest - ment a nd thorough ROI analysis should be carried out. It's important to consider ROI for both profit and shareholder value (possible sale). The return should be analysed against the return from comparative investments and thus the timing of the return considered. However, many strategic initiatives don't typically generate a yield inside 18 months so short-term thinking in this equation should be avoided. The risks against other initiatives

should also be reviewed as well as the lifecycle of the invest   -
ment and return.

Objectivity is critical; many businesses have failed because the leadership has too much ownership or passion for their own 'bad' ideas and not enough listening to the river's flow and learning to spot the good currents (ideas). An investment panel and decision-making process also increases shareholder value as ideas become tested, simply and quickly around an agreed mechanism. Board members nearly always have very different risk profiles and energy is lost via debate rather than analysis. The analysis forms part of the equation. Great entrepreneurs develop this by instinct and this should not be ignored in the decision-making process. I am just suggesting that both spec -
trums - analysis and instinct - should be utilised in decision making, with increased objectivity on whose idea is right. In business leadership, there are no wrong questions, only unasked ones. Without asking, we cannot listen to and receive answers. It is your responsibility to ask. No one else can do that for you.

Thinking like an investor may also require you to be clearer on when to say no in order to ensure focus. I have noticed that many leaders are rightly optimists, but this often makes them easy to sell to. Many strategic initiatives come out of enthusi -
astic sales or agenda meetings where the persuasive outsider over-influences the strategy – no, no and no! I call these initiat -
ives 'kites'; they might look as if they will fly but they have a high risk of blowing away. If you are considering something new, how much is it relevant to your business design, purpose and destination? There are some quite dynamic businesses held back because the Managing Director is not totally clear on the direction, and this is where such external influences easily

knock them off course. Stay clear of kites. Stay disciplined and keep focused on your course.

Looking ahead

I am looking forward to my hydrogen-fuelled driverless car to take me to meetings. I will still insist on old-fashioned meetings as reading body language is essential to negotiation success and increasingly I have found people using body language overwriting filters. En route I will acquire some more tree planting credits, for pleasure, via the net – I enjoy the live webcam forest feed of my previous investments. I no longer shop for goods or food as my computer and fridge automatic - ally maintain my stock for me and, further, I have lost interest in consumerism despite being a capitalist. Instead I spend my time being a humanist (human self-choice morality/awareness) and tackling the environmental and poverty gap in the vacuum left by the decline in religious belief. Next, en route, my 'voice book' translates my client call to Growth Africa (previously Kenya) into Swahili, after which I close my eyes and the car anticipates my favourite meditative light/sound mood environ. Look, I don't know, and I may already appear outdated (the super-rich are already much closer to this lifestyle), but what are the big picture consumer/client trends and how are you future-proofing your business design to account for them?

- *Objectively how good is our intelligence?*

- *How good are our analytics and research resource?*

Being busy incrementally improving profits, operations and recruitment are all important parts of the strategy, but they are the 'managing' parts and should not be confused with the 'lead - ership' parts. Incremental strategy rarely creates shift changes, and often it can result in 'busy fool' syndrome; that is, too busy doing what you have always done because your habit, history and plan tells you it's right, rather than what you need to do to future-proof the business. Interestingly, many business plans are lengthy reiterations of today, lacking vision about new initiatives and new ways of doing things. Often they talk about goals without identifying the inputs required to achieve them. The concept of By Design is to create a business structure that gives leaders free space to spend more time to gain, via research, the right intelligence to create better decisions and navigate a clearer, more effective strategic course and, in its achievement, look forward to where the market is going – not where it has come from.

- *What new products, acquisitions, strategic alliances and routes to market should we consider?*

In effective design, we have no predetermination that controls what we are or what we do, and we are radically free to act independently of influences. Therefore, we can create the business, purpose and values we want through our choices. We can create the businesses we want by design. So the leading premise of By Design is the idea that we should put aside the past and present, look at the future and 'play' with being absolutely radical. I am not suggesting by the way that we all completely disband the current activities, as incremental initiatives still have a firm contribution. I am, however, suggesting that for strategic work, the less beholden we are to history and short-term needs, the more insight and the better design and strategy you will ultimately achieve... openness and flexibility as opposed to narrowness. What structure should we aim at, who are truly the right people to work with, and where is the market going; how do we align our services and products ahead so that the market drives demand?

Summary

In Business By Design we lead rather than manage, and we are beholden to the past only in analysis, in research and in under - standing the currents and flows. Through quiet determination and with absolute belief and focus, we navigate – little by little – a better, more intelligent and easier course, sharing and leading. We have no predetermination that controls what we are or what we do; we make the difference; we create the busi - ness, purpose and values we want.

Chapter 2
Purposeful leadership in the river

Introduction

In this chapter, I pose questions and ideas to make your role as a business leader more rewarding, more purposeful and deliver better results. Effectively, what 'outlook' can leaders best adopt in today's fast-moving rivers to maintain purpose, clarity, confid - ence and energy?

Listening to the river

Your role as a business leader is to define the business purpose, and effectively set the course in the river (the market), so that you and your team can navigate safely. The river is constantly in flux with lots of hidden currents, white water and dangerous rocks. If you have ever done white water kayaking or rafting, you will know that the key to successful navigation is to be utterly clear on your course, anticipatory, focused and listening and feeling every movement; so it is with business.

It's very difficult to navigate intense white water when you are running fast downstream and any good kayaker or rafter knows to look for breathing space in what are called eddies. These are serene pools where the rocks or bank jut out and the water is gently pushed away, creating a movement of water counter to the main current. The safe eddy enables you to rest calmly, to plan and map the course without having to fight the current and the turbulent water. It gives you space to look ahead and decide on the best and easiest course for your busi - ness. If you are constantly fighting the water rather than flowing with it, which takes planning, you will get constantly exhausted.

I see, therefore, that the role of the business leader is to seek serenity in order to plan and navigate a safe course – once that course has been set, to then get into the flow of change by listening and tuning into what's working and what isn't and, from time to time, resetting the course for a new, safe eddy, helping and nurturing the team and business through the market.

- *Where is your eddy – your quiet calm time – so you can choose your course ahead?*

- *How much do you and the team flow with the constant flux and turbulence?*

When setting the course, I also believe a business strategist should ask two key questions "is your river (your market/the future) too turbulent?" and "is your boat strong enough; have you got the right business model?" There are many examples of exceptional corporates that have chosen to leave sectors in order to become something totally different. 3M, the Post-it Note guys, originally owned paper mills (low margin/high capex) and they morphed through choice into a product innova- tion business, ultimately selling or closing the paper mills. Nike and VW both moved from being manufacturers to brands.

The quest - creating and sustaining new habits

To achieve strategic understanding, clarity and purpose, leaders need to seek strategic calm time and look at their habits. As a business leader you will have many responsibilities and pulls on your time, and you will have developed a set of strategies and habits to deal with your work. However, the areas where you invest most of your time and energy are typically the areas you are good at and enjoy; yet what you don't enjoy or what you struggle with may well be where the biggest energy is being lost in the business. The most effective way to improve the business is for you to fully understand your current preferences and time focus and what habits these have formed. This is not about changing yourself or building new skills, it's simply about making informed choices by reviewing your position, and the quest is making the right changes.

Habits are caused by your environment and can be easily tackled. The first aspect is to recognise what your habits are and the reasons behind them. The second, with discipline and conscious effort, is to replace the habit with an alternative. At the start it will feel uncomfortable, but the good news is that the human brain takes around 21 days to adjust or develop a new habit. For example, it is easy to develop the habit of fixing problems for people by telling them what to do, yet this can make you a bottleneck in the business as people constantly refer or defer to you. Instead, develop the habit of helping people to understand how to fix their own problems by guidance and questions.

As well as questing after new positive habits, we need to consider our beliefs and work out which ones are positive and which ones are not. What you believe can strongly influence your time focus. For example you might, as many leaders do, believe it is important to be strong and exert control yet, after a bit of time in the chair, you have probably learnt that flexibility is as important, if not more so. After all, a battle plan rarely survives first engagement with the enemy. These beliefs can be both compatible and at odds; you can choose to believe strength comes in flexibility or believe strength comes with an iron will. The point is that both approaches can and do work, and indeed it is actually possible to combine them. There is usually a time for each and you can choose. Your beliefs should not over-influence the recognition of which time is right for which approach; the business is bigger than you and you have the responsibility to be adaptable. Many business leaders, male and female, display alpha male traits and, if we revert to 'type', strength, domination and determination will appear high on the agenda but many of these traits crush consensus building and listening.

In this, we can see that leadership today could be argued to be about putting aside the ego and doing what works rather than what you believe works, or would like to work. For example, many self-made owners work really hard when starting a busi - ness because, by nature, they are grafters. They believe they are making the biggest difference driving the business, but 'doing' tends to push them to working in the business, at the job, rather than working on the business, that is on the strategy and process to seek intelligent growth. The belief is that 'hard work' is all, however 'hard thought' is often far more effective. If you are flexible in your beliefs you can then combine them and seek hard work through hard thinking – not necessarily through grafting. To quote one of Bill Gates' top ten tips: "Be nice to geeks [thinkers] at school, they will rule the world."

- *Which of your current habits are good or bad and what beliefs do you need to challenge?*

- *How much do you control your responsibilities and time as opposed to the business?*

Today, in a highly turbulent world, my observation is that the most important belief is choosing the most positive outlook. That is, you and your team have total confidence that you can make a difference and can always find ways to achieve your goals given time – however difficult those goals are; the classic business mindset that failure is simply feedback. Worry and stress achieve very little, whereas if you believe you can, you probably will – even if achievement is slow.. We are not talking about the entrepreneur's pathological optimism; such optimism very often gets in the way of listening in the face of reality. More it is a question of choosing a humble forward outlook, or state of mind: if we seek positive outcomes, we must be positive.

- *Are you stressed and worried and does this have a negative impact?*

- *When are you at your best and how can you be like that more?*

So the business leader, through practice and patience, builds inner mental control, adopting and practising flexible habits and positive beliefs. Inner control and influence then expand out directly to what you do, how you spend your time, where you focus, where you connect and how you guide your business. This outlook can seem a bit passive at first as it just doesn't feel like work, but once you get used to seeking a better internal course, it is amazing how often this translates to achieving the right external path and the feeling becomes exhilarating. The concept is to look inwards before outwards, and take total responsibility for the way you act and how it impacts others. Lead yourself before you presume to lead others. "The habits of life form the soul and the soul forms the countenance." (Honoré de Balzac)

Serving not commanding

We all know many self-centric business leaders whose world is wholly about them, what they want and how successful they are. This can be a formula for financial wealth as it makes them selfishly or individually competitive, but rarely will they build truly first-class, world-beating organisations that are sustain - able beyond them. Individual competiveness creates a narrow view, whereas generous competiveness – that is, the desire as a collective to win, not for or as an individual but just to be first in class – creates organisational momentum. Effectively, the outlook of the leader is being there to serve the purpose.

Further, if the leader's definition of success is centric to their ego, people around them disengage, consensus becomes a dream and command and control are therefore the only altern - ative. The leader is forced to continually drive rather than the organisation doing the hard work for them. By serving, respecting and helping others so they can fulfil their potential, you will usually find these traits offered back, propelling you and your business forward. In this we have the idea of the truth seeker, serving to make a difference because they have a higher purpose, not commanding because it massages their ego.

The servant leader as a concept has been expressed most notably in Robert Greenleaf's books, which are an excellent reference source for those who want to take this further.

Serving is not the same as servitude and should not be mistaken for weakness; indeed it is immensely strong. For example, making tough decisions about team members who are not performing becomes easier when you serve the organisation. Discussing performance challenges clearly backed with supportive training gives individuals the best opportunity to overcome the issues for the greater good. Ultimately, if the problem remains, making a tough decision serves the organisa - tion and individual better. The individual may simply be the right person in the wrong job, and the organisation will thrive and achieve its higher purpose with employee excellence at its heart.

- *Do you avoid tough conversations that you know in your mind and heart are needed?*

The idea of the leader 'to serve' also suits the modern specialist's world. The top talent will only join organisations where they are thanked and feel a sense of purpose, achieved via leaders who respect, encourage, listen, and are passionate about organisational excellence – not just their own individual ambitions. The leader who serves the business quietly and with humility is, paradoxically in today's commercial world, the stronger man.

- *How often do you put others first and say thank you?*

- *How much does your ego dictate your conversations and ambitions?*

The habit of calmness over certainty

Children are creative, honest, playful, joyful, questioning and inspiring. They have such energy even when they are passive;

just watch them asleep and you see both the innocence and potential. Many business leaders are overworked, stressed, tired, and cynical – especially those who are never satisfied. How did we change from those children? Why does the burden of choice and responsibilities make many of us so weary? I have a view that it is the effort to achieve correctness and certainty that creates the change. As we leave childhood a transition occurs: the demand is to act our age and stop asking silly ques - tions, and by adulthood we are expected to "know better." Effectively, we are compelled to present a 'knowing' state, often internalising doubts and questions on the way. This leaves a veneer of external confidence but the inner fear, doubt and questions remain, which is draining and wastes too much energy.

My thought is that business leaders need to get back to their inner child and not be fearful of asking questions, or indeed being wrong. Only when we accept that we don't and can't have all the answers in this fast-changing world and that this is not the function of leadership, can we truly take the time to listen to others and see more clearly the purpose and the answers. Even then we may get it wrong and, if we do, should simply accept it, learn from it, apologise, change and move on. The idea is that knowing and controlling actually suppresses innovation, creativity and teamwork, thus reducing flow.

- *How much do you have to be right, and does success have to be your idea?*

- *How calm and serene are you and thus open to receive ideas and inspiration?*

A friend showed me a clip of a child of the digital age trying to click on a paper magazine as if it were a tablet. The child tried everything, even down to eventually pushing her finger into her leg on the assumption that the finger may be broken. The point of this is in her innocence and digital age understanding, she had no idea that you had to turn pages in a physical book. You don't know what you don't know. What was wonderful about the clip is that the child was not dismayed by failure but rather enjoying the experience of puzzling it out, the journey of discovery – even giggling a bit in perplexity. Of course at some point it would be great if she asked for help, but I hope you see the idea of exploration, rather than having to know.

In this idea, the business leader achieves an inner strength and calmness in their thoughts and their external being as they are more accepting of fate; simplistic, innocent, creative and playful. Instead of energy from drive, speaking, persuasion, advising, fixing, and cajoling they create energy from a sense of calmness, listening and purpose. They become the vessel rather than seeking to be the message, which is utterly dynamic.

Strength in flexibility - go with the flow

Oak trees are beautiful – proud and strong – yet they are not the tree that lives the longest. This is because they grow large but with little flexibility and can't therefore withstand the strongest gales. The oldest and most successful trees are the pines – with the bristlecone pine at number one, the oldest recorded being 4,789 years old. Pines flex with the wind. The idea here is that there is more strength in being a flexible organisation that goes with the flow rather than a rigid one. This is difficult as we want the purpose or goals to be utterly set so that we can achieve clarity and drive in one direction. The problem is that this thinking assumes the direction planned months ago is right, but is this objective still correct when the environment has changed around you, or perhaps some aspects of the journey were not considered? Business leaders succeed better when they concen-trate on the overreaching direction and the quality of the journey as opposed to trying to enforce specific destinations; it is vital to adapt as you go. Darwin says: "It's not the strongest of the species that survive, it's those most adaptable to change." The organisms that are most sensitive to the changing season, most alert and responsive to the environment have the most chance of survival.

A global economy is a complex eco-system. If we fight the environment or try to control it rather than live with it, there will always be a battle against the odds. For example, mankind is now realising this today with the green movement; we can't beat nature but must rejoin it in sustainable ways or we will fail as a species. Most of us can now feel the 'disconnect', and therefore more and more cities are putting green space at their heart. Accept and adapt to the environment for survival. I cover this concept in much more depth later in Chapter 5, Natural Selection.

- *How do you design more adaptability and flexibility in your and your team's outlook?*

What you enjoy will be working, what you don't may not

As a business leader you are probably externally pretty confident, and you drove at promotion or growing your busi-ness to build your position to where you are. Let's be honest, however, you probably did some faking along the way until you made it, but what are you still faking? Before you can achieve the next level of business growth, you may need to achieve your next level of personal growth and that means being truly honest with yourself, what you are good and bad at, then seeking help to improve these skills or to support any deficiencies. We can't after all be brilliant at everything, and there are many who believe that trying to do so is a waste of energy. You may need to seek help here as it is often difficult to look truly objectively in the mirror as we tend to see what we want to see. Interestingly, when we look at companies in the light of the strengths and weaknesses of the leader, we often also see their preferences: what they enjoy is working well, and what they don't enjoy is working badly – it's the law of focus!

- *What do you honestly do well and what don't you?*

The Peter Principle is a business theory that all people in an organisation will get promoted to their highest level of capability, in other words until they reach their position of 'incompetence'. The only way past this is to invest in that capability, with the same principle applying to leaders being more honest and objective about their own skills and development. In the words of the great Bard, Shakespeare, "The fool doth think he is wise, but the wise man knows himself to be a fool" or, in Eastern spiritualism, "The day you think you are a master is the day you cease to be!"

- *Who points out your deficiencies and how much do you listen?*

- *How much do you accept and learn from failure?*

- *Where do you gain knowledge and training?*

Future contemplation

I will write later on effective delegation but it should, I hope, by now have become clear that the business leader needs to be inaccessible from time to time to analyse, assess, review, plan, anticipate and contemplate. To seek quiet time to understand purpose and direction is as, or perhaps more, important than being approachable (my door is always open). Here we must seek balance, and technology helps as you can work anywhere, anytime, but we must avoid being a slave to every message. This means designing a business where you can entrust your team with most aspects and empower them quickly to look for solutions, only yourself getting involved if the challenge has truly escalated. A dialogue with your team as to why this quiet time is necessary can also be useful.

- *How do you create and achieve permission for quiet time?*

- *How do you make technology serve you rather than you serve it?*

- *How do you empower the team to problem solve?*

We have already seen the idea of looking ahead in the turbulent river of change, and actively seeking calm eddies to do this, but when you are in this space it is vital that you are looking as far ahead as you can with clear sight. Think about future trends and the impact on your business. Where is your market going as opposed to where has it been? Success today has already been achieved, but tomorrow has a higher purpose that we must contemplate. Hi-tech companies intuitively know that they need good research and a strong development approach, and this idea should apply to every business. All businesses have a product or service, and markets are constantly changing as consumers change focus and competitors react. In the 70s and

80s, Microsoft had the vision of a personal computer on everyone's desk; however this was before the internet. The idea was right at the time but subsequently limiting, as Apple's smartphone and tablet revolution was far greater – who needs a desk now? The sum of human knowledge can today be carried, indexed, accessed and transmitted across the globe in seconds. Much has been said about this already, but what does this mean for your business? I contend that the pace of change will accel - erate even more, leaving us with little choice but to design more agile, leaner companies with fast ideas and fast trials – and get over it if they don't work!

At the time of writing, the Western economies are supporting an ever-aging population with governments now overburdened with debt. This means we face the slowest economic growth for 100 years, yet global and emerging markets are growing at up to five times the Western pace. What can you do to expose yourself to these markets? Markets change, consumers evolve, how much do you and your team invest in research and devel - opment to navigate trends and look ahead?

- *How do you look ahead and how much do you invest in 'ideas' research and development?*

The current is where you are at, yet the future is the oppor - tunity. The successful business leader becomes a listener and a vessel totally tuned to new ideas and trends, but also completely understands where they have come from and currently are – in essence, achieving a state of mind and outlook where every muscle, breath and thought is explorative and anticipatory. Many business leaders have lives and minds that are far too busy for this outlook, usually meaning that the ego or the intel - lect is in charge. This leads to a constant state of searching, justifying, comparing and desiring as opposed to listening and awareness.

Personal sustainability

As business leaders, I contend that we have the responsibility to anticipate and ensure our companies are fit, lean and alert so they can be responsive to change, thus ensuring sustainability. Do we not have the same individual responsibility? In the West today, one in four children will live to be over 100 years old due to improved diet and exponential advances in medical science. Most of us therefore have long lives ahead but how much do we ensure that they are quality lives? So, the river leader is fresh, seeking the simple idea of healthy body and healthy mind, which means regular fitness, careful diet and managing stress to achieve personal sustainability.

Many will turn to the gym or the diet books here. Yes, there is a massive industry capitalising on this awareness but actually I question its effectiveness. I have a client who says the gym is his best charity; the membership appeases his ego but he never gets time to visit. A typical trip to the gym would take him a total of two hours yet he could walk or run for free in an hour to achieve the same result. I am simply suggesting that you build new, healthier habits into your daily routine. How many times have you sat in traffic for 45 minutes to cover three miles when you could have walked – getting the bonus of some fresh air and a quiet space to contemplate? A simple rule for exercise is 45 minutes of some type every day.

Do you reach for the chocolate to get a sugar rush in the after - noon slump? Try fruit, which has many natural sugars – think ahead and make sure this is to hand. Sugar and other refined carbohydrates (including white pasta, rice, white bread and cereals) create blood glucose spikes then subsequent tiredness as the insulin quickly processes the glucose, causing levels to crash back down. Try brown alternatives which are slow-release carbohydrates and will keep the blood glucose more stable. Porridge or protein-based dishes like omelettes are ideal breakfast choices; salads, soup and sushi are good options for lunch.

- *How aware are you of good diet and your energy levels?*

- *Where do you plan your exercise in?*

Caffeine in coffee and tea is also guilty of creating 'highs' and 'lows'. Often it is the comfort and routine of a hot drink we seek, so switch to a herbal alternative; they can take a bit of patience but once you get used to them are just as effective. If you are physically and mentally fit you will exude energy and this is contagious, but no matter how fit you are and how much energy you have, there invariably may also be times when recuperation and rest are on the agenda. Holidays are essential. Staying fresh and working in harmony requires active management. "Rome was not built in a day" and creating exceptional companies, unless you hit the crest of a wave, can take a lifetime of work. We have a responsibility to make sure, if we can, that by managing our health we are highly energetic long-term players. "To keep the body in good health is a duty, otherwise we shall not be able to keep our mind strong and clear." (Buddha)

Investments in relationships and respect

The river leader opts for a continuously respectful stance in their role. They are respectful and thankful for their team's success and for every ounce of help they receive along the way, whether or not the help receives financial recompense. This is because they recognise that every element of help is not only a step towards a more successful and aligned business, but also in their own journey as a calmer, more generous and respected leader.

- *How much do you take people for granted?*
- *Do you show you are grateful for your role in the business?*

Stephen Covey, the personal development leader, uses the metaphor of an Emotional Bank Account in his Seven Habits series, the idea being that when you make emotional deposits (helping others), you slowly build loyalty, trust and under standing. This 'deposit' concept can also be particularly effective where relationships have become strained.

True respect or appreciation is a feeling or attitude in acknow ledgment of a benefit that one has received or will receive, and genuinely having it and showing it makes you stronger. The business leader need not only adopt this stance personally; it can also be developed systematically into a brand and business. How does your business develop a grateful outlook and mindset, not with the expectation of more 'loyalty' schemes but with a simple, traditional thank you?

Forgiveness is also an important business trait. If a member of the team or supply chain lets you down – forgive them. This doesn't mean ignore it, be soft or don't rectify the situation, but it does mean be patient, avoid bitterness, and never complain behind someone's back – play fair! I am not talking about being lapdogs, just genuinely seeing life from others' points of view, being respectful, forgiving and openly grateful for everything people do for your cause, paid or not. Ultimately, remembering 'please' and 'thank you' is only polite after all.

Generous spirit

Many business leaders rise to the top because they enjoy being the centre of attention; not all of them, but many. However, studies show that this type of approach is often too ego- driven and does not give the team space to grow and thus drive the business beyond the leader. In Jim Collins' excellent business book Good to Great, he identifies the idea that the more successful leaders are the high listening ones who have humility combined with a determination and professional will towards excellence. These leaders are prepared to be openly accountable if things go wrong and go out of their way to give credit to others when things go well. They actively seek all ideas and see themselves as idea collectors as well as generators. Indeed they often give their ideas to others so they can take the credit and build their confidence up. This takes generosity and an ability to shut up verbally and mentally.

- *How good are you at shutting up?*

- *Do you have to take the credit?*

The humility idea is easy to say on paper but most leaders believe they have to talk to communicate the concept and keep the message alive. They also believe that they need to lead this charge from the front, most of the time. They also have very busy lives – and thus busy minds – and so are usually thinking, creating and analysing at a million miles an hour, which of course can lead to talking at a million miles an hour and very often interrupting! A busy mind usually means the ego or the intellect is in charge, and therefore a constant state of searching, justifying, comparing and desiring occurs. This gets in the way of listening and awareness. Purposeful leaders don't need to exert, control or drive all the time; instead, they learn and know how to be with others, increasing listening, truthful - ness, awareness and experience. A parallel metaphor for me is in the highly capable martial art ju-jitsu, where strength is found by manipulating the opponent's force against himself, rather than confronting it with one's own.

- *How and when do you control your busy mind to increase awareness?*

Pull and not push

The law of attraction is a well-known 'thought improvement' concept; the idea being that by focusing on an aspect positively and by believing the aspect will occur, the more likely it becomes. If you are negative, then negative things will occur; be positive and positive things will occur. Essentially, what we believe (consciously or unconsciously) is possible, we can achieve. A famous example is Roger Bannister's four-minute running mile, which had previously been deemed impossible. The year after Bannister's achievement, 72 people achieved it because they knew it was possible.

Business leaders that adopt a positive belief that they and the team can, over time, make a difference, move forward, find the right way and attract more success – however difficult or long the business and personal journey. The optimism is infectious. Interestingly, positive focus can be best achieved by influence rather than persuasion, as can most things. When you persuade people they often, on reflection, revert to type as they don't have ownership of the ideas. That is why consulting – unless in high specialism – usually fails as a business change method; the advice is paid for and ignored whereas coaching and ment - oring, by asking questions and sharing experiences, creates this shift in people which leads to ownership. They reach a conclu - sion themselves rather than you convincing them. Imagine if with time, patience, training and focus every one of your team could believe they are part of a higher purpose, making a differ- ence, choosing to be positive, listening, learning and enjoying their work.

- *How much do you and your team choose to be positive, believing they can make a difference?*

- *How much time do you spend empowering people, rather than persuading?*

Summary

You, the business leader, are responsible for accelerating growth and driving change in your business. In the river leader, we have the idea that by adopting and practising better self-control 'inwardly', we achieve improved 'outward' results and flow. As Mahatma Gandhi said, "You must be the change you wish to see in the world," meaning in this context that each of us will succeed more if we strive to rid ourselves of self-limiting habits and thoughts. Listening, sharing, understanding and creativity combine to create better strategies and better buy-in to those strategies.

- *What do you personally need to change to create the busi - ness change?*

- *What purposeful conversation do you need to have with yourself?*

Chapter 3
Flow

Introduction

I hope in the previous chapters to have inspired you to purpose - fully design a better business by taking the time to seek a more in-depth understanding of your organisation through research, questions and increased openness. In this chapter, I seek to make your role as the leader, when undertaking this process, easier and simpler in style and stance – in other words, to flow.

Creating and understanding flow

Building and accelerating growth in a business requires effort, and lots of it. However, by exerting precisely the right effort at the right pressure points it is possible to contribute tirelessly and more effortlessly or 'in flow'. How do you know the right effort and points? Well, that's the mastery, but many leaders are too busy to take the time to find those pressure points, leading to overexertion and inefficiency.

- *How much time do you spend looking objectively for the right pressure points to create growth as opposed to being busy with other people's agendas?*

'Flow' is a recognised and studied state where an individual becomes fully immersed in an activity, feeling energized and focused. It is a state of enjoyment and complete engagement. It was first written about by Mihály Csíkszentmihályi, a psycholo-gist studying successful artists and their ability to immerse themselves wholly and positively in their work, sometimes to create exceptional results. In the interviews he conducted, several people described their experiences as 'flow' after using the metaphor of a water current carrying them along.

In a business context, flow can be achieved on individual activ - ities but also by engaging objectively in implementing the right strategy in the right way, making both business growth and leadership appear almost effortless. By focusing on the areas you can control rather than those you can't, by being positive, strategic and objective, and by listening at all times, business can be made fun and easier. When your thoughts conflict with reality you nearly always suffer; when you accept reality and concentrate positively on what you can change you achieve flow.

Of course talking about achieving flow and mastery can make it sound simple, but often it requires significant study and a change in approach from the leader. It may also require you to recognise your own strengths, weaknesses and habits and be prepared to adjust. Anxiety, distraction, external events and negativity all impact on flow so the leadership counterbalance is awareness, personal adjustment and self-control. Further studies show that flow can be greatly enhanced by carefully 'designing' certain environments; this includes creating highly challenging tasks, where the skills are available to deliver the result, free from distraction and with immediate feedback.

- *How well do you and your team avoid distraction?*

- *How can you delegate or reduce management time and increase leadership time?*

The idea of flow is also in the Buddhist concept of seeking a state of mind known as the 'action of inaction' or 'doing without doing'. This comparison to religion reminds us that the achievement of flow requires contemplation and patience. However, there are basics that are helpful and merely aspiring to the state is a useful process or exercise. Further, the quest for flow also aligns closely with the skill set of strong leaders. I have set out what I see as the key factors below.

Listening

Accelerating growth and shareholder value requires under - standing and that only comes with research and lots of ques - tions with active listening. Where is the market (river) really going? What do the team and customers truly think? Active listening is not just about silence as too often we are thinking in the silence about what to say next, reflecting on our views, or judging what has been said. True listening requires a blank canvas to understand what is being said without external or internal judgement interruptions, which reduce effectiveness. Good listeners understand that the skill is active not passive and it's the active ability to stay in the moment and hear the message (verbal and non-verbal) and build with appropriate, carefully phrased questions motivated by curiosity. People like being listened to and understood, they like the extra effort put into achieving this; it builds rapport and exceptional goodwill. The skill of great active listening is also very rare in a busy world and it is inspirational when engaged in correctly.

- *How much do you truly listen – objectively and curiously?*

- *How do you put aside your preconceptions when you listen?*

Empowering ideas

Taking the time out to navigate further ahead and design a better business will create a more efficient business, but you can't do all the work alone. Your team has to be involved, trusted and given the 'space' to help drive and deliver the vision. This motivation is best achieved by involvement, careful communication and dramatised ideas; that is, simple ideas and messages that uplift, encapsulate and share the goals. Many studies on leadership talk about trust, eloquence or rhetoric as being base tools for empowering; it must therefore be worth investing in carefully crafting and designing your messages.

- *How can you create a team you trust and empower them to lead the change?*

- *What time and care do you take to dramatise your ideas and craft your messages?*

Service and patience

Your role is not to make yourself look good and achieve just your own personal aspirations; great leaders know it's about honest service and commitment. It's patiently and at all times putting the result or the goal above yourself, and with commit-ment, humility and forbearance to create the change. Further, by taking the time to listen, to say thank you and to always do what you say you are going to do, you build rapport and grat-itude which increases loyalty, team integrity, understanding and support. Patience does not mean you don't want things done quickly; it means, however, that you and the team know that big changes take time to bear fruit.

- *How patient or impatient are you and what impact does this have on strategy?*

- *How selfless are you?*

Positive confidence

The aim is to be clear to the team that there is an achievable, larger goal while maintaining a relaxed, natural focus which preserves the message. Rarely do plans run perfectly. As Nat King Cole wrote, "There will be trouble ahead, but let's face the music and dance." In other words, even when things get tough (and they always will at some point) choose the positive, choose to learn from it and teach your team the same approach. As one leader put it to me, the outlook is always, "I am a believer."

- *How relaxed are you?*

- *How positive are you, however turbulent the river becomes?*

Creativity, intuition and decisiveness

Things will go wrong, changes will be required and decisions will need to be made; of these, many will rest on your shoulders. Too often, however, leaders opt for the obvious choice or make 'bull in a china shop' decisions. Great leaders have the ability to quickly step back, listen, watch, and then employ imagination, intuition and creativity. They then use advice, experience, analysis and – ultimately – their instinct to be decisive with clarity. It's important here to understand that you can't get every decision right, but great leaders usually beat the odds. They know that being decisive and sometimes wrong (after appropriate analysis) is usually better than procrastina - tion – trust yourself! By the way, if you do call it wrong, admit - ting your mistake and learning from it adds to integrity and trust.

- *Who are your mentors?*

- *How much do you rush for the quick think?*

- *How much free space do you give yourself to allow for creativity?*

- *How much do you listen when sharing the burden?*

- *Do you admit and learn from your mistakes openly?*

Challenge and inspire people

Challenge people in a positive way, which encourages them to reach higher than they are used to. Help them examine their stretching aspirations and align them to the organisation. Encourage, nurture and support your team to set and reach for progressively more ambitious goals. Acknowledge achieve - ments and say thank you. Commend hard work consistently to inspire, even if people are financially remunerated well. A consistent gratefulness builds loyalty and inspiration. Investing in people and training builds loyalty. It is your job to motivate and that begins with aspirations for people and an appreciation for their contribution.

- *How much do you thank and commend people, even for the ordinary things?*

- *How do you set stretching goals for your team?*

- *How much do you or your organisation systematically invest in people?*

Exceptional communication

Great leaders clearly and succinctly describe their aspirations, plans and consequently the actions they are seeking. Relate your design and vision to your team effectively and you will ensure you are all working towards the same goal. Clarity requires repetition, focus and simplicity. This takes time invest - ment, which is best summarised by Samuel Johnson's famous quote, "I did not have time to write you a short letter, so I wrote you a long one instead."

- *How much time do you take to ensure people know what you want, where you and they are going and check to ensure they are truly clear?*

Flow through the team - democratic decisions, autonomous solutions

Creating a strategy may not be the hardest element; imple - menting it successfully can be more difficult. Often this is why the leaders get forced to overexert themselves, and get stuck in the 'hands-on' management space, driving the team and the strategic change but reducing flow. Why is that?

Where implementation is difficult, it may be because the team is poorly structured or the ideas are beyond their current skill sets, but often it is also because the leader is too far ahead in the river and the team can't see how or believe they can or should catch up. In the modern world, employees are usually better educated, have more choice and access to more informa - tion. With this in mind they won't buy in to the strategy unless they have contributed to its inception and understanding. This means that in order to build consensus, the strategy should be worked and adjusted by the team and alternatives should also be considered with the team. Effectively, once you have done your research and development and can see a new route down the river, you share it with the team and workshop it. Done right, this 'democratic' process will usually bring about improvements, but more importantly you will secure team buy-in. Of course this takes longer but, with buy-in, the team will implement changes autonomously which is far faster.

- *How can you involve your team more?*

- *How do you build consensus behind the purpose?*

This method does involve group thinking, which is a skill in itself, particularly making sure everyone gets a voice, including the introverts. Introverts won't contribute as much in meetings and often perform better with pre-meeting analysis and feed - back, whilst the loudest, most charismatic voice is often the least thought through.

- *How well do you facilitate?*

- *How do you ensure the introverts get a voice/contribute?*

Group thinking is about creating change buy-in, but it is vital to make it clear you understand that whatever the final strategy set, you – the leader – will still take ultimate responsibility for its success or failure. Many employees will be cynical of group thinking so you will also need to set the scene in reminding the team of their obligations to customers and employees to engage appropriately. Finally, when engaging in group thinking, it is important to discuss with 'all' the biggest mistake of 'all' – that is, not trying new things.

- *How do you show your ultimate responsibility, do you play the blame game?*

- *Do you try lots of new things and accept they can't all work?*

In summary, appeal to the team's sense of purpose and decide where you can democratically build consensus to improve, and then build trust with the team to implement it autonomously. This method creates flow, shares the work and creates buy-in with faster change despite the fact that decisions take a little longer. It remains critical even with team-driven change to carefully track and monitor progress to maintain accountability.

- *How accountable do you make your team?*

- *How much do you track initiatives?*

Personal discipline and motivation

The river will always have white water; the strategy will always need adjusting, there is constant work, there are challenges, adjustments and adverse weather. I have seen the constant flux and turbulence of strategy literally grind leaders into exhaus - tion. Every decision ends up being made out of worry, cynicism or fear which usually leads to failure. The belief that there are no problems, only challenges and opportunities, is the critical attitude to create flow, and to think good thoughts requires effort. Effort requires self-discipline and motivation to manage your energy levels and outlook, ensuring willpower and persist - ence.

- *How much effort do you put into managing your outlook and persistence levels?*

The word discipline actually comes from the word disciple, which is where a person is taken to be trained in a code, order or craft. This should help remind us that self-discipline and a positive outlook require significant investment and training; the awareness that in spite of negative circumstances or emotions, we insist on keeping going to achieve the goal even if it requires sacrifice. Failure is not an option; no matter how many setbacks (learning opportunities) you have, practice makes perfect. Inter-estingly, I am not sure that school (which is where most of us train) is a great grounding for self-discipline. Educational discipline is usually too highly imposed to learn fully the self-discipline of choosing and controlling your own outlook. Therefore, where do we learn it?

- *What training have you or your team had for self-discipline?*

Self-discipline is an action, so it is actually stronger than motiv-ation, which is an emotion, as a source of strength to see some-thing through. The power to deliver large and exceptional undertakings when you say you will is awe-inspiring. Its achievement is, overall, a learned skill coming from training, breaking the mindset into chunks, managing your energy levels, and patiently building to the end result. Working smart, choosing the right tasks and tools all contribute but, ultimately, success is still achieved by tackling things task by task and staying the course. There is no talent to acquiring discipline; mastery requires effective management of the mind, awareness, focus and practice.

- *How clear are you on breaking down the goal task by task?*

- *How do you stay positive with the end goal in mind?*

Mentors, skills, knowledge and education

Knowledge is power. You will be aware of the phrase that there is always someone richer than you (at the time of writing, it's Bill Gates again at £73 billion); at the same time there is always someone wiser. Today, the world is highly complex with many specialists, and it is impossible to be expert in all areas.

To achieve flow, therefore, we cannot expect to be expert in all elements, apart from perhaps designing and choosing the right team – which includes mentors, coaches and specialist advisors. To be successful at this, we need to ensure we take the time and care to research and invite the right team to share their thoughts and ideas on how they can help. In particular a mentor or coach is a critical tool. It is almost impossible, when you are in the white water of the river, paddling hard, to see objectively where your inefficiencies, improvements and errors lie. A good coach or mentor will hold the mirror up and dramatically help you improve and identify the right goals and your knowledge; they will also save you time by ensuring the correct focus and helping you avoid pitfalls or mistakes.

A coach and a mentor will also focus on how to improve your communication, listen more effectively, reduce stress, simplify your agenda, and maintain motivation. The right experts will also free your time up and increase your confidence in the journey or course you are navigating. Confidence will help increase the attraction of your navigation to others.

Being clear and simple

Business can seem like a tangled web of complexities. For those immersed in every element of the detail and analysis, to try to fully understand the drivers and make the right decisions, it can seem very difficult to communicate this to others, simply, but that is what we must do.

Leadership trust is built when complex ideas are brought to an absolute: that is fresh, clear and simple; a point which your staff, customers and market can understand, relate to and implement. If you carry the clutter of 'your' analysis and 'your' journey, how will you create a simple brand of wisdom that generates fellowship and leads? Fifty-page plans and long PowerPoint presentations create barriers to simplicity.

- *How much do you reduce complexities and say less more powerfully?*

- *What do you really want to say/need to say?*

- *How do you say it quickly and effectively?*

- *What is your simple and essential brand of wisdom?*

- *How can you say it differently (memorable form) and repeat, repeat?*

Creating inspiration, encouraging motivation

As we get more responsibility in any business career, the naivety tends to disappear. We mature but, perhaps, more often than not we become more cynical and conservative as the knowledge creates awareness and builds fear. I don't urge anyone to be reckless but to achieve flow we must strive to be more curious, relaxed, open, playful and positive. Who would you want to follow – the world- weary wise or the positive, curious and exciting sage?

When I have discussed this with people, they have said to me that you can't have good days every day, things go wrong; I try to be positive but it's tough out there. If life is a journey on the river and we are simply part of that journey, can we not find the inner peace to keep positive and curious regardless of the chal - lenges? As I wrote this, I thought of myself as a child. I had no limits; I could be whatever I wanted. I had no hang-ups (people are generally nice to kids), I could daydream when I liked, ask what I liked, and was generally excited by everything – after all, everything was a discovery.

Yet, everything still is a discovery so perhaps we need to stop taking ourselves so seriously and instead carry the inspiration of children playing every day. Do you know and can you describe how an iron ship floats, how binoculars actually work, why we invented civilisation, where your colleagues go on holiday? Turn off the bad news; instead keep discovering, learning, engaging, having fun and you will always be fresh. Add listening, respect and lots of thanks and you have an inspirational outlook which drives motivation. People will want to leap into the river with you.

- *Where do you imagine and explore?*

Why aren't more people like this? It's a great question but I suspect the answer is this: it's too easy and, in a complex world, we can't believe it's that simple.

Belief

Do I believe business flow is possible? If you believe it's possible, then it's possible. I am well aware that this chapter has a hint of 'New Age', but I hope the logic of what I have said shines through, and helps at least to question and challenge your outlook. If you can learn flow you will have more time, less stress and be stronger and more fun 'in the river'. We can then navigate without being bound to any given course, and learn to take things as they come, changing what we can. We reduce anxiety and remorse, and instead love, laugh and create.

The Ernest Shackleton Antarctica expedition in 1914 demon-strates the power of leadership flow. When his expedition on the Endurance encountered serious trouble in January 1915 and became trapped in pack ice, he had to reinvent the team's goals and flow in the direction that fate set. Exploration became rescue. For months, the ship was stuck in the ice but Shackleton insisted that day-to-day duties continued, from swabbing the decks to scientific tests. He kept the team busy, thereby redu - cing the potential for high anxiety in what was a precarious situation, whilst praying that the ice would thin so that they could continue the exploration. The *Endurance* held for months but the pressure of the ice slowly crushed the timber ship and, in October, the water started pouring in. Now, camping on the ice, previous plans became irrelevant and Shackleton set a new goal: "Ship and stores have gone — so now we'll go home." Miles from shore, stranded on the ice, many of the team signi - ficantly doubted their ability, but Shackleton carefully contained their opposition (concentrating on the doubters by assigning them to his tent and work party) and won them over with his constant courage, attention, communication, confidence and enthusiasm – even though the situation was grim indeed. Again, Shackleton looked forward and established a new team routine in the camp whilst waiting for the ice to break – impro - vising, adapting, hunting, fishing and using every resource at hand.

The men finally took to the lifeboats in April 1916 and, after a week of seasickness, dehydration and surviving the storms, they reached Elephant Island – deserted, but land nonetheless. Immediately, Shackleton planned the next goal and took the largest lifeboat with five other men on a perilous journey to South Georgia, and then on to a whaling station and civiliza - tion. During the next few months, Shackleton set sail in three different ships to reach Elephant Island and the rest of his crew, but none could cut through the pack ice. Finally, in August 1916, aboard a Chilean steamer, Shackleton rescued the 22 remaining men. "I have done it," he wrote to his wife Emily. "Not a life lost, and we have been through hell."

In any review, Shackleton's original planning was flawed as they set out against advice with heavier than usual ice but, once in crisis, his approach was extraordinary. Setting goal after goal with extreme determination and unswerving belief in the flow and their capability to innovate and ultimately succeed – despite grim circumstances and with the odds against them – Shackleton innovated and inspired with each step, conversation, action and goal. His team knew, in no uncertain terms, that whatever came before them on the ice, their leader would not give up, would do his utmost to bring them home alive. Shackleton shows us that self-awareness, belief, positivity, adaptability and commitment are the key to leadership success in fast-moving global markets. Further, that creativity and purposefulness create exceptional results.

Summary

If, as business leaders, we take the time to create the right environment and adopt the right outlook, with the right effort at the right points, it is possible to contribute tirelessly, more effortlessly and with more enjoyment – resulting in 'flow'.

Chapter 4
Ahead

Introduction

*To effectively navigate the river we have to see and be ahead.
Markets flow and change, and thus our strategy needs to be flex -
ible. To achieve this in a structured way we need to set a course
on how we think the river will be 'ahead' – anticipating the
future. Further, we need to set where we aim to be in the future –
the goals. Finally, how can we navigate ahead better to create
competitive advantage? In this chapter, we explore these three
concepts: how and why we should anticipate the future, goal
setting and ensuring we are ahead of our commercial competi -
tion with a talent, service, brand, or products that give distinc -
tion.*

The future

The river is in constant flux and, therefore, whilst the past and
present have defined us today, we must look ahead to 'own' the
future. Essentially, as leaders, we must learn to anticipate and
trust. By anticipate, I mean take decisions based on where we
believe the business will be as opposed to where it is. By trust, I
mean acceptance of the speculative and uncertain time and
research costs needed to create the intelligence, analysis and
instinct to anticipate in combination with expertise.

As a leader you intuitively know to anticipate, but far too many leaders are drawn wholly into managing the day-to-day with the result that they fail to truly see where the river is going when setting business strategy. They therefore miss opportun - ities and can end up fire-fighting. As a simple example, very often we see organisations where people's skill sets are just not up to the next level of growth. This is often because they were only recruited for and trained for today, with limited input into future 'next-level' training. Yet where businesses systematically recruit and develop their people for next-level skills, fast-track growth is more often achieved. In other words, if you want to be successful in the future, then you need to build a business based on future likelihoods rather than today. Thinking ahead also reduces pressure; for example, diarising key renewal dates six to nine months in advance gives you ample time to think hard at the renewal solution as opposed to the usual deadline rush. Understanding shifts in your environment and trends means taking time out from the day-to-day to dream and ponder.

There are many who dismiss the future as impossible to 'predict' and so they spend little time worrying about it. Certainly predicting singular events is difficult; however, ignoring long-term market 'trends' creates flawed strategies. Trends intelligence tends to show the likely future market current. For example, the internet has swept away many tradi - tional media and is bringing a broader global outlook with the sum of human knowledge at our fingertips. Surely this means that the pace of invention will further accelerate as the basis of ideas is easier to share. The speed of the last 200 years of inven - tion has far outpaced any other time because we had literacy and printing. 3D TV (nearly ready for holographic) is magic when looked at by someone born in 1850, yet it is simply the evolution of photography. Medical science has been succeeding in extending life expectancy by two to three years for every decade, which means that many children born today can expect to live for 100 years. Think about it – in their ten decades, another 20 years will be added by medical science; of course this will lead to density issues in cities and the many challenges that come with that. These are trends and they are statistically easy to analyse if you look at the past 'tracker' data. This data can thus provide the foundations of a future mindset and a basis for thinking ahead and for acting as a leader rather than a follower, generating foresight in the course the river is likely to take. When leaders actively engage with trend material, data and evolution they can understand its significance and explore new avenues and options.

With time investment and thought, the future becomes more visible and opens up to us. Interestingly, we can also realise that the present is actually being led by the future and we can use this to effectively set better current strategies. This reduces stress, increases options and creates competitive advantage. As leaders, the more you study the future, the more likely you are to be able to make the right decisions.

Some leaders anticipate relying on instinct as opposed to analysis, and this is dangerous – but at least they do anticipate. However, it is better to make predictions based on intelligence and data by building a toolkit and resource to receive this information. Further, as the main check in most businesses is the financial or investment team, any 'anticipation strategy' the leader develops is far more likely to pass the financial check if backed by some substantive evidence or data supporting the strategy. It is interesting that most private-equity backed busi - nesses surge as they generally employ 'numbers men' who also understand analysis and investing as opposed to saving.

- *Where do you gather evidence for your strategy?*

- *How do you create an intelligence system that ensures you are ahead?*

Gut feel or instinct has a real place in anticipation but should be backed up by careful research. Of course this is about balance as some also get overly caught up in the micro analysis, and we must also avoid too much emotional ownership of past strategies. They either worked or they didn't and we must instead work out what we think will work as opposed to dwelling on the past. As in earlier chapters, this is about being more relaxed about our egos. Of course to many this is intuitive and implicit in the word 'leaders', who – as people to follow – must themselves be ahead, but it is worth exploring and articu - lating so you can reflect on where the balance of your thinking and strategic time investment is.

Goals

By being clear to the team and the company about where you want to be in the river and why, you create flow and momentum towards that objective. However, setting the goal without agreeing the actions behind that goal is counterpro - ductive. The usual CEO language might be, "Our goal is to be the leading seller of commercial X in Europe." Now what does it take to achieve this? A goal should be ambitious but ultimately, when broken into steps, clearly achievable. Each step should be within reach, usually on a stretching goals basis – that is, with each goal more progressive than the last.

- *What specific actions are needed to achieve your goals?*

There are a myriad of books and articles on goal setting, so I will keep this section short. The most interesting aspect for me is that once the destination is set there is the need for step actions. It's fascinating that today in most high-performance arenas, it is 'the geeks that rule the world'; by that, I mean those who analyse and get into the detail of each micro step and action. I recently watched the highly successful motor racing film Rush, centred on the rivalry between racing drivers   James Hunt and Niki Lauder during the 1976 Formula One motor-racing season. Niki is portrayed as almost dysfunctional in his focus, breaking down every element, action, preparation or goal with very clear discipline. As a result of his 'no stones left unturned' approach he was, without doubt, the more successful although Hunt – the archetypal playboy – was, by instinct alone, perhaps the better driver. He did win the Championship once against Lauder, but far more via luck than plan; Lauder was   F1 World Champion three times in 1975, 1977 and 1984 and is considered to be one of the sport's greats. He has endorsed the film as highly accurate, and the story shows how consistency and preparation reap greater and more consistent rewards than flair alone. This concept is explored heavily in Mathew Syed's book Bounce where he reminds us that the right coach, right place and 10,000 hours of practice or more will nearly always win over talent.

Setting the goal around your primary purpose and objective and relating it to your customers' needs and your values with a future orientation is important, but today's sub actions and preparation, combined with discipline and utter focus, are what actually drive the success. Actions can be either leader-driven or team-driven but each should be clearly achievable. Goals with actions that are unachievable are demoralising, not aspirational – meaning that setting the actions and agreeing their likely realistic achievement with the team are essential. It is important to be realistic about how much time the day job takes up when agreeing timescales, as some teams can be overoptim - istic about tasks or goals because of their enthusiasm, without taking account of other activities and available resources.

You may have noticed that I have avoided the overused busi - ness strategy concept of 'visions' and 'missions'. A vision is where you want to be and a mission is how you will get there. Both are useful, with the difference in meaning clear in theory. However, in management communication, they can overlap which starts to get confusing and can therefore cause debate. It is better instead to communicate clear, simple and specific next-step goals, the reasons why, and the actions required to achieve them. By creating a culture of setting aspirational goals, breaking these down into bite-sized, measurable chunks, working with the team on the action to achieve each chunk and then consistently ensuring the delivery of the actions steps, you usually guarantee overall achievement and success. Work out the inputs and the actions, and the outputs come. If change and evolution are inevitable, then being clear on controlling the sub actions gives you control of the overall flow.

Competitive advantage

Finally, in 'ahead', we have the concept that you can design your competitive advantage carefully against likely future trends. The business team and customers will drive growth for you if the design or the strategy is ahead of the competition with a service, brand, or products that are desirable and give distinction. We need to take the time to design this position.

Rarely are businesses one of a kind so, how can they stand out as 'ahead'? They can't unless their leaders take the time out to adopt or develop differentiators. This requires careful research of both competitors and market needs. What makes your busi - ness unique in your hierarchy so you can target your sales effort more successfully? We all enjoy thinking we are better than the competition and therefore rarely do we take the time to actually look hard enough at them, but if you break down the competition's actions, the key sales strategies they employ become more obvious. This is all about research and mystery shopping. Once you have this analysis, it becomes more obvious how you can create a unique 'ahead' sales strategy with clear, stand-out and sustainable positions.

The excellent book The 22 Immutable Laws of Marketing (Al Ries and Jack Trout) extends further our understanding of unique propositions. Their first Law is that the 'first' in any category is usually most successful; however, this can take total inspiration and – dare I say – luck. That is why their second Law has the most exciting connotations for business leaders: if you can't be first in a category, then invent a new sub category. You can't be first with a fish and chip takeaway (it is an English thing), but you might be the first in your town with high-end, restaurant-style fish and chips with premium pricing and the ability to bring your own bottle. I share this example as in my local town in the UK, the new style has just appeared and already one of the old takeaways has closed.

- *How can you be 'first' with unique ideas in your sector?*

Many businesses do develop differentiators over time, through evolution and essentially via trial and error, but the process is ad hoc and often led by the marketing team in window-dressing style. But to create a truly effective foundation we must look at the overall architecture and design of the business and take the time out to design from the bottom up a niche business where demand in the niche drives the growth. Trial and error can be an effective way to fine hone the business but fast selectivity is crucial, adopting the stand-out 'ahead' material and ideas that work and changing the weak ideas that don't. Selectivity also means utterly understanding the marketing concept 'lose in order to gain'. You can't please every customer; there are way too many bandwidths of wealth, needs and tastes, so being systematic about defining your customer and saying no to others is critical in the 'ahead' concept. Usually only by choosing and seeking to own 'select' customers or segments can we create the perception of being ahead, and ultimately gain the competitive advantage.

Have you ever been into a fashion shop and then walked straight out? Was the feel too expensive, too cheap, too young… retailers are a really fascinating and very tangible way to study how some businesses choose their target sectors and adopt the 'lose in order to gain' principle. In an old business legend, a salesperson was disappointed to lose an important sale after much work. In discussing the matter with the Sales Manager, the salesperson shrugged: "I guess it just proves you can lead a horse to water, but you can't make him drink." The Sales Manager said, "Let me give you a piece of advice: your job is not to make him drink, it's to make him thirsty." With the right strategies you can increase the customer's thirst.

- *What niche can you own?*

- *Are you too broad, and if so what can you lose to gain?*

It may be that your design is not that 'radical', and that's fine, but ideally the perception in the customer's mind is that of your uniqueness and a stand-out 'ahead' position, where you are first to come to mind. Sometimes, simple tweaks in many areas can achieve this 'ahead' position with that extra level of attention to detail and the sum of the parts creating uniqueness. Interest - ingly, research suggests that to drive growth, you ideally need to be perceived as in the top three to five brands in a category. Your product may not be better but as long as the customer perceives it to be better and it fits their needs, you will drive growth.

There is perhaps a little of what is known as the 'law of focus' in the 'stand out and be niche' ideas here. If you are clear on the direction and where you can stand out, you avoid fighting on too many fronts. The Nazis proved in World War Two that despite having by far the best trained and most experienced troops, if you are spread too thin and on too many fronts you eventually lose. Most historical observers agree that taking on the Eastern Front with Russia at the same time as engaging in both Africa and with the Allies in the West was their undoing. Interestingly they nearly got away with it, but indecision due to lack of concentration, as opposed to failure, resulted in minor but telling delays in the Blitzkrieg at Stalingrad (just 50 miles from Moscow) which had always relied heavily on speed to win. With the hesitation, the Russians ground the Germans to a halt, and history finishes the story. It probably wasn't the resources but the hesitation as a result of fighting on too many fronts that eventually halted by far the best fighting machine in the world at the time. In this we can see that it is vital to be clear on which direction you should take and where you can concentrate. It may mean leaving other directions until later in order to create a genuine and clear stand-out position.

When we discuss the 'ahead' concept with many business owners they struggle. First they can't see how they can stand out today, let alone create a first-in-class 'ahead' position, but it is fascinating, when you look at and workshop each component of the business, what you can discover. Nearly every business has some key and often very positive differentiators; it's just that they are taken for granted and not given momentum or talked about. We have discussed that the perception that you are ahead is often more critical than the need to be actually ahead. One way to achieve this is by looking more clearly at what your differentiators are and actually repackaging or posi-tioning them so that each component looks different, then communicating the difference cohesively across the organisa-tion. That is to say, the website, the sales team, customer services, letters and marketing material should all clearly show the stand-out differentiators. You don't need to say a lot, just say it more effectively. I am not suggesting by the way that component differentiators are the only way to be ahead. Bold strokes are rare but highly important.

- *What are your best-kept positive secrets (hidden differenti-ators)?*

- *How much does your business communicate its differenti-ators clearly and succinctly from sales staff to reception to website?*

Let me give an example. Maybe you are an estate agent, one of many in the town, and you sell on your expertise and marketing (they all do, and I know yours is better but the customer can't tell); so it's hard to stand out ahead. Hard but highly possible by design. Most agencies have a fast and high success rate so you could, for example, guarantee to halve your fee if a sale is not agreed in two months; further, agree an extra 0.25% on the sale fee but include a virtual video tour and a bespoke designer brochure. Finally, you offer a free dressing advice service to help people to prepare the home for sale, perhaps with referral schemes to decorate. When you are pitching for the house sale, you package this as a central theme – for example, 'one step further' – then you drill and drill and drill your sales staff to repeat the mantra, so that the whole business, from the website to the negotiators, is clear on exactly why you go 'one step further' and why you care about it. Here is an agent leaving no stone unturned and starting to be aggressively proactive. I am not saying, by the way, that for an agent all these initiatives would work, it's just the point about component differentiators creating an overall, unique 'ahead' position with an overriding central theme; then ensuring that every communication and employee is aligned relentlessly and over an extended period of time behind this.

- *What specialism can you 'own' and truly walk tall in?*

Summary

In summary, the river business leader looks ahead, setting goals, adopting first-in-class yet specialist differentiators and both adapting to and spotting trends to determine a better course. If leaders spend more time on researching and looking ahead enough in the river, they will come across unique differ - entiators or concepts – ideas that can be built within an organ - isation's creativity and culture. Once you have the ideas, set the marketing, the organisation and the design around them, drive at them, and the more you focus on them, if they are right, the easier growth becomes. You will have an 'ahead' niche that will in itself drive growth rather than you having to drive it every day. This process should create competitive advantage, client loyalty and a calling.

Chapter 5
Natural selection

Introduction

In this chapter, I use the comparison of natural selection to help leaders understand how to navigate and adapt successfully to the business environment and wade through complexity. The idea of natural selection, introduced by Charles Darwin and Alfred Wallace, states that organisms with favourable traits to an environment are more likely to succeed. Success (survival and health) enables these organisms to then pass on these traits to the next generation, and over time the trait subsequently increases in frequency in the offspring, resulting ultimately in evolution of the species. Exactly the same can be said for companies; that is, the businesses that understand and select the successful traits, and deselect the bad traits, thrive. The role of leadership is to be at the head of the selection process, creating dynamic, sustainable and thriving organisations, utterly adapt - able within their hierarchy.

Complexity

On many levels, business leadership under the microscope becomes very complex and as this complexity increases, so does the challenge. We have to assess our future trends and align ourselves with these; then we have to get the right team doing the right thing at the right time and in the right way, with the right marketing, infrastructure and pricing. All this ignores the corporate governance and legislative pressures. No one aspect of business is complex, but it is achieving the multi-level synchronicity that makes it so challenging and yet so exciting. In Chapter 2, which covers purposeful leadership, I have suggested that more time needs to be spent on contemplation to create understanding as multi-level complexity requires significant time investment, which is why you need to design your role around leadership (time light) and not management (labour intensive). Then again, on another level, business is really rather simple. A Business Studies student asked me what the secret was to successful business. Looking for a simple answer, I replied: "Consistently earning more money than you spend and making more right decisions than wrong ones."

The complexity is fascinating; how did business evolve to become this complex and is it too complicated to encompass all aspects in any one mind or small team? To an extent we have to understand that, at a micro level, to learn, understand and analyse every skill and metric would be an impossible task. However, what is vital is an effective, simplified dashboard of key performance measures - one that enables us to quickly assess the right traits, patterns and movements in the business complexity and then select the right approach.

Natural selection is not in any way random. Those variations which give greater health and reproductive success in nature are retained, and less successful variations are weeded out. When the environment changes, or when organisms move to a different environment, different variations are selected, leading eventually to different species – and so it is with companies. If however, as leaders, we are to influence the selection process, we need to build a toolkit that helps us understand which traits to adopt and which to reject, and we need the time to study.

In a recent conversation with one of the United Kingdom's wealthier men (£650 million on the last deal alone), I asked him what he considered to be the secret to his business success and he suggested that it was voracious reading. He read, analysed and questioned from cover to cover every single report for five or six hours a day. This is extreme, of course, but I hope you take the point. In order to complete the analysis of what is working or not working, and thus to 'select', we need to have access to the right performance analytics on our businesses – quickly and reliably. Effectively, this is about creating the time and a system to analyse, review and seek understanding.

- *How do you understand what works and what doesn't, select the good and reject the bad?*

Performance dashboard

To measure initiatives and performance is not as difficult as it sounds. Every business has, at its core, key performance indic - ators that are relevant. If you think of your business analytics as creating a dashboard, like your car's, you can usually create a system that gives you the key analytics on one screen or piece of paper. Most companies fail to achieve this due to the disjoint between their platforms. That is the disjoint in creating a converging analysis between their financial data, sales data, marketing, production and IT data. They also fail to take account of the vested interests their teams may have in avoiding sharing the data transparently. Does the sales team fear that marketing will get bigger budgets to their detriment, or vice versa? Is the IT department worried that if the system becomes too efficient, the company will no longer need someone to run it? This is disappointing, but let's face it – no one likes to be under the spotlight. However, we must as leaders tackle the vested interests to achieve transparency. Transparent data and analytics are crucial to understand which 'genes' or people, products or strategy to select. If you don't 'select', the market environment will, and this may not be in your favour. The whole business needs to get behind simple performance measurement in the pursuit of excellence and to enable the selection of successful traits to ensure survival of the fittest.

Having the right, timely and accurate performance metrics is vital and well worth the money. It's better to slow growth until you can measure the drivers correctly. As a leader, unless you understand what strategy to select, you can't make clear decisions quickly, and indecision creates significant growth drag. The right measurement and dashboard help you to communicate – quickly and clearly – traits, targets, processes and expectations and, in addition, share why. It is important that such targets and processes are not just outputs but also inputs; for example in sales, the number of calls that are needed and the reasons for them, not just the financial sales target; or in marketing, what is your cost per acquisition of a client against your average sale? You can't expect improved results or output without changing and selecting the right inputs.

Identifying, measuring and, importantly, coaching to the right performance metrics leads directly to behaviour change and skill improvement across the entire team. People don't always do what is right on an output basis, even if they are seeking the best result, as the inputs are not always obvious, so being clear on what inputs are required to drive growth is essential. My favourite example of inputs that are not obvious is in fitness training. It used to be thought that lots of continuous exercise was the right way to build fitness but science (measurement) has shown us that a mixture of fast and then slow, or 'interval' training as this type of training is called, is far more effective. Fast and slow training builds faster lactic acid resistance and aerobic capability, but it is not in any way obvious and, to a certain extent, appears counter-intuitive – yet the results in performance prove the method. You can slug it out to get fit but it's harder and not as smart or efficient as the less obvious input of bursts of fast and slow interval training. Once the team understands the 'smart' and sometimes less obvious activities they should concentrate on, they can focus in the right direction and against clear objectives, which gives the leadership the ability to evaluate – training and coaching in quantified activ - ities and approaches.

Statistically, the majority of business leaders are 'big picture' in character type; that is, they are creative, intuitive and charis - matic as opposed to being driven by data and attention to detail. This is fine as long as the need for attention to detail and analysis is recognised and the right support is recruited to create the right dashboard and system for its creation.

Once the system is in place, even if you only spend an hour or two a week studying the dashboard, I guarantee it will speed up your decisions and understanding, reducing the chance element of selection. It is critical the analysis is convergent, covering all the disciplines and objective metrics. Have you noticed how the Finance Director's report is always pessimistic and the Sales Director's optimistic? Design an objective dashboard that is checkable.

There are a myriad of ways to create a convergent performance dashboard and to thus achieve higher understanding in the analytics. In today's world, the Cloud is often embraced as the right way to head for most businesses, particularly as there are more and more providers offering convergence data systems, for example combining sales CRM with financial management.

- *How good is your system in creating clear, simple perform - ance analytics?*

- *How much time do you spend seeking to understand the data and trend patterns?*

Key performance reports

There are some great books and systems on the market to aid you with the right analytics to select better traits and make better decisions ahead of the market. One key shift in the dash - board for most companies is the trailing tracker concept; that is, to get the date, month-on-month, over a longer period than a year, typically two, so you can compare last year's same seasonal period to this year's – for example month against month per product-type sales or lead generation. This really helps in seeing the trends and ironing out seasonal fluctuations.

My basic structure of the key performance reports is:

Financial: Trailing tracker, measuring turnover, gross profit, and overhead and operating profit, over 24 months on one sheet. The tracker enables you to use month-on-month direct comparison to the previous year and thus see overall seasonal trends and long-term cycles. Further, a daily cash position and monthly cash flow tracker. Also, aged debtor creditor days, and balance sheet gearing.

Sales: Number of leads, self-generated/marketing. Number of meaningful calls, number of meetings (or video conferences), number of proposals, quality of proposals, conversion rate to meetings, average sale and Gap per sale. Further, the number and regularity of follow-up calls including quality of notes and record keeping. Sales per employee, per salesperson.

Marketing: Per campaign investment cost, per lead cost, volume of leads directly against the campaign, number of clients secured and thus cost per acquisition per client, against average sale. By measuring the return on investment and cost per acquisition of a client you can select which campaigns to keep, and drop the lower performing ones, then use the freed-up budget to trial new campaigns. Understanding how much it costs you to win a client enables you to start growth via marketing programming. "If we run a campaign and scale it up, we will win X new clients which, in turn, generates Y." It's amazing how many see marketing as a 'soft creative-led skill' whereas marketing should be driven by the maths first, or the 'hard analytics skill', with the soft aspects following. If you are engaged in branding, such as sponsorship, PR or exhibitions, be wary as these are areas where it is notoriously difficult to track response. Of course your marketing team should also be monitoring all the sub sets, such as internet or email campaign clicks, speed of response to clicks.

Production: Quality assurance, conformity, cost per unit, time per unit on delivery, lead time, waste reduction, inventory, capacity utilization.

You will also need to monitor delivery time, client loyalty, complaints, standard employee metrics, including employee retention rates, and new hits.

The IT system should be designed, and I contend that no effort should be spared to achieve this, to create a coherent, simple dashboard or picture of the above in a couple of pages (and no more) showing where you are, what is working and what is not. Armed with this you should be able to run your company from anywhere in the world, without material effort or subjective employee input. The right system will also achieve this without reams of statistics and labour-intensive research.

- *How convergent (one place, all disciplines) is your dash-board?*

- *What period does your tracker cover and is it long enough to see the boost and lags outside of seasonality?*

Standards, processes and goals

With the right performance dashboard, we can understand and select the ideas and activities that work and can design repeatable processes that free up time and enable us to be more efficient and sustainable. Earlier in the book, we discussed the idea of flow with the key element being efficiency. In most organisations, the effort that is wasted because of misdirection is extraordinary; this is the Pareto principle, named after an Italian economist. The Pareto principle is based on the idea of the 80-20 rule. This is a common business principle, much observed (it's also surprisingly common in nature - 80% of peas come from 20% of pods!). For example, in most businesses 80% of your sales comes from 20% of your customers, 80% of complaints from 20% of customers, 80% of sales made by 20% of sales staff. Behind the principle we can thus see the idea that by 'selection', many businesses can create fundamental shifts by focusing on the most effective areas and eliminating, or systemising, the rest. If, for example, 20% of your customers demand 80% of your time, this is not necessarily the most profitable activity. Therefore, selecting the right customers strategically and saying no to the wrong ones is a critical example of selection. The 80/20 principle is not always proved by the data but at its core remains the idea that, with the right dash - board, you can see where the wasted effort is far more effect - ively and you can then select the process, standards and goals to create efficiency.

The process is the series of designed and selected actions or inputs that you and your team have chosen in order to create the most efficient result. The standard is the benchmark you set around the quality employed in its engagement. The goal is the realistic change you wish to see. The management might design the process and engage the team in its activities but the leader - ship checks that the process or activity is correctly selected and heading in the right direction on the river. It is the joint responsibility of the management and the leader to ensure the standards set are unfailingly met. When failure does occur, this may mean the activity or process is wrong, but it also may mean that there is a weak link either in clarity, training or personnel. Review, clarify, coach, train or deselect where the team fail to hit reasonable standards. You can't grow a business without appraisals and rigorous insistence that performance benchmarks must be met; that is, the leadership must set and continuously demand and track high standards. The environ - ment you design is also critical where people recognise and take pride in the importance of sharing and maintaining the standards and there is reward for doing so both in gratitude and remuneration on a sustainable basis.

Overall, in the principle of natural selection, we have the ability to constantly improve every aspect of the business via constant incremental gains in selecting the right traits. Of course, as in Chapter 1, we should not ignore other specific initiatives such as strategic alliances, new products or acquisitions. These initi - atives are vital for long-term radical shifts in growth. However, with the right analytics backed by the correctly designed processes and standards, which are constantly evolved to improve efficiency, we create many simple small steps that lead to long-term growth. Usually the fastest gains result from the incremental 'selection' of the right activities, processes and improvements within the core business. Michel Gerber, in his series of *E-Myth* books, describes business systemisation as the genesis for gain, and the dashboard enables the leaders to select and design the right systems, ideally implemented and monitored by management.

I want to spare a thought for the start-up entrepreneur reader. You may not yet have management or many staff behind you yet, but you will be aspiring to it, so the natural selection concept remains important. The more you systemise and benchmark your business now, the easier it will be to grow.

- *Who champions and shares your standards and how do you monitor them?*

- *Where is your organisation inefficient and how does it adapt to efficiencies?*

Sharing selection

Selection and the dashboard are the leader's responsibility, however much can be achieved by sharing the concepts with the team so that they ultimately have the ability to select and adapt, within reason, without guidance – although it is important to recognise that this selection does not encompass the overall strategy, otherwise you will have empowered chaos. This is similar to the Japanese management principle of Kaizen (good change) – the core idea in Kaizen being that you humanise the workplace to eliminate over-hard work and train people to perform experiments and innovate in an observed way to improve processes and increase efficiency. Kaizen is selection on a continuous basis, usually at a more departmental level. Much success in creating lean manufacturing processes has been achieved with Kaizen, but it is just as applicable to all industries and services. By setting the aim that the team has a responsibility to work smart and select the positive traits, you set a culture that encompasses continuous change enabling the business to drive adaption bottom-up as well as top-down, resulting in transformation.

- *How much do you have a culture of 'selection'?*

- *Does your team understand the importance of selection and engage in a regular process to achieve it?*

Selection workshops and facilitation

To create team-driven selection, regular workshops are useful. Remember to ask the introverted beforehand for their improve-ment ideas as they may not speak up in meetings. It is not necessary to be able to do the job or process that you are trying to improve, simply to be good at facilitation and encouraging creativity and lead with questions like, what have we missed, what is causing constant difficulty, and what feels like hard work? It is important that these discussions are non-judge-mental, fun and in a comfortable, creative, free environment without distraction, perhaps away from day-to-day work. Further, facilitating these workshops is about securing particip-ation, innovation and buy-in as opposed to the leadership setting the agenda.

By creating a business which is designed to adapt to its environment via intelligent selection, as opposed to fighting its environment, you ensure survival, dynamics and usually growth as well as increased shareholder value. Interestingly, when selling a company (my day job), I am often asked if a business has been through a pre-sale preparation, perhaps with the question in mind of whether the business has been overstretched in the process. Far from it, buyers prefer businesses where the team is dynamic and positive about change and used to natural selection. Such companies are easier to expand; imagine buying a company and trying to expand the business from a highly static conservative base. Studies show that over 70% of acquisitions fail due to the inability to change, manage the people and merge cultures.

- *How comfortable are you with letting others drive the ideas?*

- *How can you create a culture of selection and adaption?*

- *Do you listen more than talk?*

Summary

In the natural selection concept we have the metaphor of the leader as the Darwinian biologist; that is, measuring and testing scientifically against a well-designed performance dashboard and then selecting what works. By reviewing the performance indicators and testing, the leader can then remove the rocks from the river (waste) and finally the gravel (inefficiency) and dramatically improve the speed of flow and ease in the business. You can, with the right internal and external research and performance indicators, understand the environment more effectively and select the good ideas, processes, people and initiatives more consistently whilst simultaneously deselecting the bad ones to achieve a culture of positive evolution and progress.

Chapter 6
Creating adventurer teams and change

Introduction

In the previous chapter on natural selection, we have the idea that it is the most adaptive and selective companies that are successful but, to achieve this, you need agile teams: adventurer and explorer teams that rapidly and proactively self-select what is working and cease what isn't, adapting quickly to their envir - onment.

Leaders are usually not there to manage the status quo but to set a course for ambitious, accelerated growth. In this course, traditionally, the leaders carry the team with them but instead how do we get the team to drive the evolution and growth? Teams that are dynamic, adaptable and responsive to change in their environments in a proactive and lean way consistently outperform. To add to the metaphor of the book, let's call these adventurer teams: a team with no limits and a 'can do' proactive mindset. How do you create teams with this adventurer outlook, particularly as, in my view, getting people to do things differently is the number one challenge – after identifying direc - tion – that leaders face. Generally people are not dynamic, with perhaps the majority being risk averse and motivated by security rather than ambition. They might complain about being bored, or worry about their lack of promotion, but are they really prepared to adopt the changes or take the risks that

are required to fulfil their personal or their organisation's ambitions?

Business leaders often have to set and drive major changes to
the course, which with conservative or ill-informed teams can
lead to isolation, frustration, and deadlock on both sides.
Increasing a team's awareness of the requirement to adapt at
source – that is, sharing why the change helps the team deliver
the new course – is highly effective and reduces executive
burnout. Most leaders believe change ensures security because
it influences the environment in their favour, but many
employees perceive change, leadership and entrepreneurship
as risky as there are no rules and the sought course is
unchartered territory. Of course business leaders and owners
do have rules, both legislative, competitive and the ones they
and their shareholders set, but beyond these boundaries
leaders can set their own moral and strategic compass.

It is this ability to decide and lead in the way you want that
makes business leadership so exciting. You set the direction and
there are – if you really stop and think about this – no precon   -
ceptions or foregone conclusions as to how far you can go.
Civilisation in itself is one great modern change experiment, we
invented agriculture some 9,000 years ago, then came the
barter system and finally money. Money itself has evolved from
bags of coins to printed notes, now to plastic and ultimately,
within the next 15 years, to purely electronic. I have no doubt
that e-money will lead the way eventually to one global credit
currency. The point is that once you get people living in large
groups (only possible with agriculture and money), sharing and
creating new ideas becomes inevitable and unstoppable, just
like a river's flow. Today, change is unmistakably faster than at
any other point in the 200,000-year history of modern man,
primarily due to the innovation of printing, and now the digital

revolution, batching and leveraging ideas in real time. Leaders need to spend time with their teams, discussing and examining the 'real-time' change challenge or fast-flowing waters at source.

In the fast-flowing river, leaders invariably have, or need to adopt, a greater sense of adventure but they can struggle to communicate this with their teams. In my opinion, this is because they discuss the task or 'content' as opposed to the 'context' in far too much detail and too quickly; that is, the majority of conversations are focused on the 'what' to change as opposed to 'why' change. This mistake leads to an inertia dam as people struggle to see the impact of the course change or the reason. Worse, many organisations correctly insist on repetitive consistent delivery of procedures, but this – by encouraging conservatisms – actually encourages the dam. So, you have decided you are going to change course; you face a dam; the old, trusted gun-to-the-head leadership method is not allowed. What next?

Context not content

The best way to flow past or even to remove the inertia dam is by sharing more effectively the dynamics of the market and the competition, and thus the need to be adaptive. Consistently share the context of change, the market drivers, and then combine this with involving people – thus increasing the sense of adventure and adaptability.

Implementation

Change by consensus can take longer to secure but the great news is that often even a bad decision implemented well can outperform a good decision implemented badly. With the team onside and with clear deadlines, accountability and tracking jointly agreed, implementation can usually be extremely quick and better team-driven as the team realise the need for change to ensure continued success. Sometimes, of course, change may result in redundancies or redeployment but the process should still be the same. The needs of the organisation are far greater than any individual and an adaptive approach will inevitably mean that people may have to be moved or redeployed. It is better to get this clear in the culture and people used to the idea, however unsettling. The leaders need to take a calming, listening approach and do what they can to protect people whilst being commercial about what needs to be done. In this respect, one of the biggest challenges for leaders, directors and owners is that it may be necessary to impose change on people who have become friends. Sometimes the friendship can result in leaders avoiding the important conversation which, invari- ably, adversely affects everyone in the long term. The river leader will put the organisation first and the need to evolve and get better above friendship. Face-to-face communication is fundamental in big change projects as emails and notices just don't deliver the right level of personal attention to ensure understanding, nor have the required calming influence. Once a change path is set, keep reiterating the results. In this we can remember parts of Chapter 2: that we are there to listen and serve the team without ego, regardless of the change outcome being sought.

1. Little by little; change management

- *Are you realistic about your time frames for changes and how anticipatory are you and your organisation in the changes?*

Creating and delivering effective change is a key part of busi -
ness leadership. The leaders set the brief by designing the
culture and insisting on an autonomous team; independent,
free-thinking and entrepreneurial, expected to be creative,
innovative and sharing best practice in the day-to-day.
Recruiting people with awareness of change cultures and who
by nature are dynamic will help create this culture. Interest -
ingly, many leaders will design the hard elements of a business
but rarely do they take time to design the soft elements. This is
essentially designing the team and organisation's mental
outlook via agreeing and defining values. There have been a lot
of studies (in particular Tom Peters' In Search of Excellence)
which suggest that organisations that design and recruit to a
culture create stronger communities. This indicates that, when
recruiting, it's often better to look at values and attitudes
(particularly an individual's attitude to dynamics) before skills
and, if a new recruit is struggling to fit a dynamic outlook, the
person is removed or realises quickly that they are in the wrong
organisation, ensuring continued cultural alignment of the business. The team and the recruits that stay become advocates, not
because of what the business does, but why it does it and how it
does it. They become passionate and committed because the
values strike a chord, not the product. This, of course, dramatically aids long-term retention and loyalty and enables change to
become a constant, woven into the course of the business due
to the team awareness of the need for evolution.

- *How do you encourage different outlooks to inspire innova -
tion?*

Developing a high performance team takes time and invest -
ment, both in sharing information, targets, training and the
right recruitment. Sometimes leaders can try and leap before
they can walk, perhaps 'selling' the need for change or better

results, but not objectively backing this with the right strategy, resource and training. Usually such leaders hit the inertia wall. First, what is it most important to change and why change? What is the data, the analysis and where is the research? Then investigate, further research and analyse, share the findings. Then workshop to agree the changes, secure new ideas and innovate. Design carefully the new approach, replace the old with the new and insist on constant, conscious application. Finally review, then embed with training, to create consistent delivery.

- *How much do you allow preconditioning, predetermination to control you rather than determining your own thoughts?*

- *What are our options, how do we overcome the challenge, what is the best way to make a decision jointly on this?*

2. Changing entrenched minds

- *How do leaders therefore instil dynamisms in the face of the human urge to conservatism or security, and still maintain reliable task output?*

Most people inherently understand the need to be open to change in their lives or the workplace but lack the motivation to change. It's easy to revert to task or previous habit and uncon - sciously encourage the inertia wall. This is not necessarily conscious resistance but passive inertia that makes delivering new ways and new initiatives harder to establish. The leader finds the conservatism of the team slows the current almost to a standstill with the water so clogged it's impossible to wade through, let alone move quickly and create flow. We have all experienced the challenge of setting new methods and embra - cing new ways – it is not easy. Many of us make it more difficult than it should be, often lamenting the old way because it was familiar, not because it was better. For example, a recent survey by global accountants PWC found that over 70% of CEOs cited that their acquisitions failed to match expectations due to change management and cultural challenges. All the money on acquisitions is spent on legal, financial and commercial due dili - gence but very little is invested in managing the cultural trans - ition, management change and people, yet today it is possible to do psychometric tests, reputation audits and a whole host of other team review analysis.

Dynamic 'change' organisations can be designed; the best way to build one is by adopting evolution awareness as part of the organisation's cultural foundations. Far too much effort is put into 'selling' the change in order to implement it, rather than first creating awareness about the need to evolve, adopt and adapt – effectively teaching how to learn before teaching specifics as to how or why change or evolution is necessary. We can recruit to a change outlook as well as train, which ensures the foundations of dynamic adaption are inherent in the culture.

Leaders can create flexible outlooks by example. That is, never lament the past but simply learn from it, reduce ego and over-dogmatic strategic ownership in favour of embracing flow; look ahead and talk ahead rather than dwell on the good old days. Train yourself to embrace new technologies and ideas and continuously dedicate time to their research. In this respect, the digital age is both a curse and a blessing. With the internet, the sum of human knowledge is at our fingertips (and, with voice-activated searches already here, what next?) and the seeming effect is to have accelerated complex business change. A genuine global market accessible to even small businesses is one example, or the ability to establish a virtual business very quickly. This is both a threat, because it means we must be ahead, but also, and more importantly, an enormous oppor - tunity. If you are lean, if you are fast, if you research, if you listen, if you and your organisation flow, how far and fast can you go? The world is what you think it is, and by immersing yourself in a forward-thinking approach, you will create an innovation outlook and experience in both your life and the organisation. Decisions, feeling and actions are based on this 'think' innovation and adaptive outlook.

Leaders have a responsibility to share this outlook, to design and set the culture of the organisation, particularly in respect of delivery and adaption. At the heart of every culture should be personal and organisational responsibility for delivery, but behind that, an awareness, desire and positive mindset to an adaptive approach. There are of course lots of books on the specifics and theories of change management, but mostly these assume one specific initiative. However, we are examining here the concept of creating an overall fluid organisation, with many parallel adaptive approaches being undertaken, both micro and macro, preferably even being driven by the team as opposed to the leader. Of course one way is to build from the ground up a dynamic, high performing team and we can look at this premise in the recruitment section of this chapter; but what if you or someone else has built the team already and have an estab   -lished business with players who have become rather stale? (It's not your fault by the way, it's human nature in combination with the organisational need for reliability). Or perhaps you have just inherited a stalled business via acquisition, succession or promotion. What do you do?

For me, the first step is for leaders to learn patience. Invariably, leaders – either by self-appointment or promotion – are gener -ally more dynamic than the rest of the team, particularly the entrepreneur owner. This can often lead to tension and frustra -tion; they find themselves asking: "Why don't they work as hard as me?" "Why are they not self-motivated?" "Why are they so conservative?" Frustration completely undermines high performance; instead leaders should adopt a patient teaching approach and bring an awareness around the need to be adaptive and to change, to evolve and thus to thrive. It is your job to show people the course and to help them build the skills to accelerate them down the course. Predominantly this is a design exercise. First, it's about getting the right people in the right roles and second, it's about designing a coaching and training machine to ensure and support awareness of the need for dynamics and adaption, as well as exploring and building clearly on the motivation people need to encourage them to embrace new products, ideas, innovations and to test different ways of doing things.

From understanding what needs to change and why, comes exploration – workshops, group brainstorms, research and investigative analysis. Options are explored with the team and leadership, then pros and cons reviewed before jointly choosing a path. You may have personally decided on a path before the team's involvement, which is dangerous as it can undermine the consensus process where all see the exploration as a foregone conclusion. This is often translated to a feeling of having been manipulated, undermining critical trust in the leadership. Worse, the leader's preconception may be wrong as they don't necessarily understand all aspects of the business as well as the team who may be more hands-on and immersed in the real challenges. Certainly the strategy or suggestion should need to openly survive interrogation to be jointly accepted. If leaders have possible solutions they should be presented simply as options, not conclusions. Oversold conclusions typically make people more obstructive; the mindset the team settles on can be that this change will benefit the directors and owners, not me, so I will not cooperate and might resist and obstruct this change.

3. Clarity, confidence and energy

- *How face-to-face are you?*

An important aspect of ensuring continuous evolution, as well as teaching awareness and employing best consultative practice with the team, is anticipation. A business can be hard to steer or change direction, and the larger it is the more true this might be. This is why most corporates employ silo principles, creating lots of innovative micro businesses within the whole. But of course the more you research, the more you see ahead and the more you can anticipate for effective navigation and start creating the movements earlier. The unsinkable transatlantic liner Titanic sank in 1912 because she was moving too fast, her rudder was too small and the iceberg she hit, whilst spotted ahead, was not seen in time to avoid damage to one too many watertight chambers for her to remain afloat. In other words, it's usually a combination of factors that causes problems rather than any one thing, but anticipation and looking further ahead reduce potential disasters. The key is to effect change, even though it is a proactive rather than reactive change, well before it is necessary, despite the advantages being less immediate. Change usually takes longer than initially anticipated, so be patient and set realistic timetables. In particular, people can tend to be overoptimistic about what they can do; tracking and accountability therefore remain critical to the process.

- *Who is responsible for what? How do we ensure that all are clear on the agreed change before tracking and re-enforcing such change?*

4. Communication and tracking

- *How patient are you with others?*

With time, patience, the right investment and the right reward structures, you can create a high-performance team, dynamic and adaptive to change, rewarded by successful adoptions and innovations. High performance means a team that consistently delivers or exceeds the target, with clear roles and comple - mentary skill sets; aligned and working together on a clear set of goals; focused, committed and determined. The team works in partnership; collaborating, sharing and communicating to exceed the goal, to spot adaptions, and to overcome hurdles. It is important that it is the team rather than any one individual that is driving the performance and that the team is playing to its strengths and offsetting its weaknesses with a strong mix of people to ensure dynamic viewpoints without conflict, and with trust and accountability to deliver. Effectively, the team feels a strong sense of joint accountability to innovate, try new things, be adaptive, set goals and drive growth. The leader designs the team and ensures that a forward-looking mindset, flexibility, and embracing adaption are at the heart of the team values – all this, together with clarity and highly evolved roles and respons - ibilities.

- *What's the data, why they need to make the change, how accurate is the analysis and what have we missed?*

5. Cultural versus commercial balance

- *How much have you set, designed and insisted on the organisation's values?*

Designing an awareness culture around the need for dynamics together with a clear, simple process for delivering consulted change quickly will drive the design of the business, with the team and individuals bringing in innovations and improve-ments unaided. This will help deliver growth and accelerate competiveness, increasing business flow – efficient improve-ment without overexertion. You and your management will have to ensure optimum delivery and be ultimately accountable for this process and the results. It is surprising how little sense of personal accountability is inherent in some people, so you may need the usual performance reviews; appraisals to assist with your teaching and servitude in delivering a better organ-isation. There are, of course, a myriad of techniques and approaches to 'performance' management. I can't cover them all in this book but I will share one simple idea for the leader: insist on the highest standards and demand absolute excellence in performance. Too many leaders cut too much slack in this area, delegating and assuming delivery without checking. Make it clear that exceptional standards are a given, check continually that they are delivered and deal fairly and firmly with any fail-ings. If a team or individual consistently fails to deliver fair and pre-agreed standards, then they are insubordinate, incompetent and needing training, or incapable (when training has failed). Set the standards and training, support and nurture and develop an environment where the standards are unfailingly met. To create the necessary culture – high standards, adaptive, evolutionary – you have to ensure that you have the right people in the right roles with the right support, values and absolute clarity. 'Think' the quiet leader, but one with absolute determination to achieve continuous improvement and first-in-class benchmark standards.

- *What standards do you set, how high are they and how accountable do you hold people to achieving them?*

6. Right team, right place, right motivations

- *How accountable are your team to try new ideas?*

Nowadays, particularly in Western cultures and especially in highly skilled and specialist business arenas, teams are created via consensus and involvement. Rarely does the autocratic manager succeed as, in today's competitive employment market places, employees have choice and their loyalty is intrinsically linked to their involvement and values alignment as opposed to command and control. To create an adaptive selective change culture and maintain high performance, leaders will typically employ an open decision-making style, combining data analysis, future trends, research and instinct. Further, they will have open communication and designed communication and feedback methods with regular reviews. Leaders should also avoid the 'mini me' trap and insist on diversity, designing methods of feedback and contribution for all types of thinking and communication from introverted to extroverted, logical to passionate. They should put in significant effort to ensure that the different styles then work cohesively. Of course a team made up of one 'type', who all think similarly, will often have less conflict or confusion but, to drive growth, diversity should be designed and instead effort put in to ensure cohesiveness, aligned values, flexibility and positive, exciting environments.

Leaders should not confuse a consensus approach with being weak. They may still need to have tough conversations. Many business leaders avoid performance conversations for fear of disruption, but then later live to regret it. If someone is under-performing, it is your duty to choose conflict over harmony and redress it, whether by training, performance management or ceasing the contract. Further tough conversations may benefit the consensus building. Intense debate and perhaps arguments can be a reflection of passionate teams that care. An excessive need for harmony can restrict 'productive ideological conflict'.

The leader's role is not to stop the debate, but to make sure that people do not take it personally.

- *How diverse is your team?*

- *How well do you and your team balance reliability with a change outlook?*

Summary

In conclusion, set high standards, add flexibility, strong communication, investment and focus and you can enhance the culture to accelerate effective growth.

Chapter 7
Creating and realising value

Introduction

The questions so far have examined the leader's outlook, with the idea that fresh questions enhance both strategy and leadership, confidence and flow. We have also looked at the fact that by being ahead of the market and with a more team-driven approach to management, leaders gain and, in a rapidly changing world, need more time to effectively be entrepreneurial. This enables them to develop the business in the most effective way, usually via new territories and products, research, and possibly exploring acquisi - tions – all with shareholder value in mind. The ideal is, perhaps, the creation of a wholly team-managed business, where the leaders are then operating in pioneering areas, which should achieve more growth and ultimately become more profitable and valuable – navig - ating more effectively the rivers of cash. Throughout this journey, we have examined that purpose is as critical as success and, there - fore, we must also look at the difficult question of when enough is enough. Building and realising business value may – and probably should – be a part of the goal and certainly considered carefully in the business strategy. The financial wealth achieved in the world is mainly capital wealth, not income wealth, and in the business leader's journey, achieving and ultimately realising business value may become a critical part of both business and personal navigation in the river.

Creating value

Most business owners focus purely on profit in their strategy, and only create shareholder or business value as a 'by-product'. This is missing an opportunity, but also perhaps misses a core question in our journey and in capitalism: how do I know when enough is enough? When does capital certainty outweigh income risk, and perhaps time wealth become more important than financial wealth? The majority of wealth in the world is 'capital' driven not 'income' driven and creating and realising shareholder value can be focused upon as a primary strategy. At its core, behind this idea, lies a simple question when making strategic decisions. Instead of asking the usual question, "Will we make more profit as a result of this strategy?" we ask a further question, "Will the strategy enhance our shareholder value?"

This concept influences both the leadership's outlook and the specifics of the strategy. There are some strategic decisions that may be highly profitable, but make minimal impact on the value of the company. Focusing on winning more buyers remains firmly entrenched in the idea that recurring revenue is where the true value of goodwill lies. I could write a whole book on the subject of creating shareholder value but the basic ingredients of the recipe are actually fairly simple. Companies that follow the recipe, whatever the sector, will be the most valuable. Values will differ a fair bit per sector but overall the ingredients can be applied broadly.

The recipe combines the following ingredients. Add good recurring revenue, preferably contracted; this ingredient brings sustainable, forecastable cash flow, which is eminently fund - able. Operate in a niche, preferably global and rapidly growing with barriers to entry; the barriers are usually expertise, intel -

lectual property or brand strength and positioning. This ingredient adds opportunity whilst reducing competitive threat. Finally, add the ingredient of a market, customer and team-driven business. Companies are more valuable when the product and positioning create the growth in combination with the team, rather than the owners meeting the demand and driving the growth. Of course there are many other aspects, the 'seasoning'. Ultimately, the buyer's taste will judge how good the recipe is but, with preparation and the right strategies, leaders can significantly enhance that attraction. Such strategies might include, for example, reducing risks such as overreliance on one customer or supplier, or having manage - ment in place capable of working with a buyer to secure next-level growth.

How can you 'design' the business to enhance value?

Like many business initiatives, the design for value takes time to create. For established businesses, it requires detailed analysis of what's working and what isn't. A quality dashboard will enable you to understand where the opportunities to gain optimum performance are, plus careful research to position the business ahead of the market demand, rather than chasing it. Typically, carefully researching and creating the right plan to design shareholder value into the core of a business can take three to six months, and then two to five years to instigate. Much advice on the subject of securing business value talks about 'sale preparation' taking at least three years but this advice is usually about sprucing up the dish for sale by securing good data, better visual presentation, enhanced corporate structure, better systems, removing pitfalls, and tightening up contracts to add to buyer visibility and confidence. I am suggesting going well beyond sprucing up the dish and that, as leaders, we design the business for sale from the start and place this thinking at the heart of decision making. When making decisions, asking "How will this impact on business value?" should be a key question. With the opportunity to both design shareholder value from the start and prepare for it pre-sale, we are moving into the arena of specialist advice and it can be helpful to work with professional advisors closely and early on to maximise the opportunities and add perspective.

With the outlook that shareholder value is inherent in every key business decision, we achieve a higher quality of understanding and can see more clearly which strategies and decisions 'fit' the plan and journey. This adds to confidence, clarity and energy. We may influence value significantly or only a little but the pursuit creates better informed decisions, and even small changes in every area of the business can add up to a big differ-ence. Imagine a ten per cent improvement in your recurring revenue, training, delegation, customer loyalty, team motiva - tion, systems, marketing, buying arrangements, office presenta-tion, accounts management ... all these combined might add up to 100% increase in shareholder value. Many shareholder value strategies are good business practice anyway, and you don't always have to apply them as a prelude to sale. They can be used to give you the choice to sell, even if, when you face the decision, you may choose not to.

Valuation

In creating shareholder value it is useful for leaders to have a broad understanding of how businesses are valued, although professional advice should always be sought. As I have explained, acquisitions should also firmly be on the leader's agenda so understanding how businesses are valued is again helpful. Private companies are hard to value as their shares are not quoted. The final value is only obtained by the final sale price, which is dictated by the buyer's perception of desirability, comparative investments, risk and the net assets of the busi - ness. However, value is possible to estimate, typically by assuming the perception buyers will have of the business and relating this to the sustainable adjusted net profits generated.

The profits are deemed a good measure of the goodwill in a business. Typically, adjustments are made to separate extraordinary costs and owner's costs to create a more accurate measure of the profits. Most valuations in private companies are carried out utilising a pre-tax price earnings multiple ranging usually from three to ten times profit. The higher multiples would usually have stronger profits, high recurring revenue, and significant economies of scale in fast-developing markets. Bigger profits usually also push the multiple to the higher quartile, as they appeal to buyers with deeper pockets. Business leaders should seek advice on valuations specific to their sector and strategy. It can be helpful to model the potential value of your business based on your expectations of growth; that is, seeking to understand how large your business will need to be and what profits you will need to have to support shareholders' value aspirations in the future. The idea here is that we gain a better understanding of what the return on investment from our strategies might be on a capital or share - holder value basis. Essentially, we are using the creation of shareholder value as part of the decision-making process both personally, if we are key shareholders, and as business leaders.

The above gives a basic guide to valuations. However intellec - tual property and brand positioning, combined with scalability, are having an increasingly heavy influence on valuation and these aspects are subjective and almost incalculable, increasing the complexity of valuations. Another complexity is that deal structures are usually not straightforward and rarely are they all cash, with buyers typically now hedging risk via 'earn-out' structures and deferred payments. Not only does this 'hedging' reduce the buyers' cost of capital, it links the deal to future performance, which is ultimately what they are buying. The structure of a deal arrived upon will have significant bearing on the valuation calculation.

Finally, the above valuation methods assume a 100% sale but minority shareholdings are usually discounted (unless in floated markets) as they have less control in a business. With all these complexities and subjectivity, a good advisor can be an invaluable guide, and the shareholder value plan is often won well in advance of the realisation with the right advisors.

Timing

Creating shareholder value can be central to the leadership role but with this also comes the responsibility of leaders knowing what is the right type of exit; that is, how best to realise value and when is the right time. Some 75% of exits today are via trade or private equity sale because other exit routes are much reduced: flotation is now reserved for larger companies due to the cost; management buyouts (MBOs) due to funding challenges and risk; and family succession due to educated sons and daughters seeking their own path. All this combines with retirement longevity forcing owners to insist on better terms than family or management can afford. It can also be argued that competitive pressure is increasing the need for trade companies to be positive and aggressive about acquisitions, as opposed to just relying on organic growth. Securing an acquisition to obtain economies of scale and synergy can help trade buyers secure their own shareholder value and help them scale-up more rapidly than organic growth can achieve. This speed, scale and opportunity is driving acquisition demand, both with trade and international buyers.

What type of exit best suits your business or organisation?

The right time will depend on the type of exit and it will depend on the business's cycle, the market's perceptions and the share - holder outlook.

When is an exit worth capitalising on versus the aspirations of the shareholders versus the market's perception of value?

This is an alignment question and a key part of the leader's role is in analysing and securing this alignment, which can be very challenging. Usually I find the alignment falls at a crossroads in the business journey. The first route into the crossroads is that the likely sale value is deemed to have met the aspirations of the shareholders for capital wealth, effectively when enough is enough. The second route is where the business is still growing with prospects possibly better utilised by a larger corporate entity. The third route is where the next cycle of investment is around the corner and thus the next cycle of business is being faced, along perhaps with the objective reflection of whether the leaders and the shareholders are the right stewards for this next cycle. The final, fourth route into the crossroads is the market perception; that is, securing an optimum sale outside of economic forces and where the market is viewing both acquisitions and your sector favourably. If all routes meet we have our crossroads and the time may be right.

The crossroads is often a narrow point in time and can easily be missed, so the role of the leader is to navigate ahead and anticipate the crossroads. Missing the crossroads can mean losing the optimum value and, with business running in cycles, typically the next crossroads may not occur for five to ten years. For example, the business may need to reinvest heavily to capture the next level of growth in the next cycle, and once this investment is made it takes time to secure return on investment, reducing the prospect of a sale for the duration of the investment. In seeking to anticipate the crossroads as I have mentioned in earlier chapters, leaders need to create roles that give them the space to research and think ahead of the strategy rather than being wholly immersed in managing the detail and doing the job as this reduces the time and opportunities for looking ahead. Anticipation requires reflection and a hands-off rather than hands-on approach. Securing the timing of an exit correctly can be highly lucrative and far more tax effective than creating income wealth, as tax on capital gains in most countries is far less than corporation or income tax, which usually combine to high rates. Capital well invested can also secure excellent rates of return, often with less risk than running or owning a private company.

How clear are the leaders on the timing triggers for sale?

Overall the right time is when the company is profitable and growing, offering buyers good potential, economies of scale and a match with their strategy, probably with barriers to competitive entry due either to recurring revenue, intellectual property, brand or team expertise. Often this is when the shareholders and leadership are reaping the rewards of their efforts and they can still see continued growth. They are, therefore, perhaps understandably reticent to let go of the shareholding, but hanging on too long can be dangerous. If the company keeps growing will you be under-capitalised again and will you need second-tier management? Will the competition get smarter? Will this start increasing pressure on the business (and you) and reduce profits in future years? Interestingly, the right buyer may solve many of these pressures.

Choosing timing is not just a practical issue of analysing a crossroads. In my introduction, I suggested that business leaders and key shareholders achieve enlightenment by putting aside intellectual methods and that it is the completeness and richness of our experiences personally and in business that create understanding, balance and satisfaction. The idea here is that, as business leaders, we only achieve enlightenment if we experiment, if we learn and listen, which all adds to wealth in our positive being. Every action or event leads to under-standing, and buying or selling a business for both capital and time wealth is potentially a large contributor, which may be a significant stop-off point in your journey down the river.

Experience, realism and objectivity are critical to making the decision to buy or sell, which ideally should always be driven by what is right for the business first, and the shareholders second. It is very common to see businesses where the M&A (Mergers and Acquisitions) strategy is distorted by the shareholders' unrealistic aspirations, or lack of understanding, often driven by fear of what they will do next and poor research. I am minded of Theodore Roosevelt's famous quote:

"In any moment of decision the best thing you can do is the right thing. The worst thing you can do is nothing."

How objective are the shareholders about an exit strategy?

Predicting a buoyant M&A market is also important. The market for private companies does not seem to fluctuate as much as the corporate environment; this is probably because they trade at lower values so have less to drop, but there are peaks and troughs like any stock or property market. Interestingly the larger the business, the higher the fluctuations – perhaps relating more closely to stock markets, which also comprise larger enterprises. To predict markets, the best we can all do is seek clarity. Look at the trends. Ask for professionals' opinions. Read international and trade press. Are interest rates up? What is the legislative environment for your business? Are new technologies coming in? What are the demographics of your customers? Is the world economy growing or stagnant? What acquisitions are being made in your sector? What are the multiples?

Realising the value

When the crossroads or stop-off point approaches, the method of realisation must also be decided upon. Assuming that a sale is not via family or management succession, we are left with either a trade sale, investment sale or a flotation. Flotations tend to be more a route to finance than an outright exit and are a complex subject in their own right, so I have focused on the trade or investment sale and assumed a 100% disposal.

What is the right exit strategy for you, your business and your team?

Selling a business can be a very complex and time-consuming proposition, so even if the buyer is known, a proven lead advisor or intermediary should be appointed early on. Their cost will easily be offset by the saving in management time and expertise to avoid the pitfalls along the sale route. A lead advisor's expertise will create a competitive purchaser environment from both same sector and synergistic trade, international and investment buyers. Last year, in the professional practice I work in, only five per cent of transactions were to buyers directly known and obvious to the seller. The environment is managed in a discreet and confidential way, releasing data carefully to increase buyer understanding on the company for sale, and further enhancing the proposition by careful positioning. A good intermediary will also have a hand in both preparing the company to enhance shareholder value and helping leaders anticipate the sale crossroads.

We have discussed earlier that valuations are subjective. A buyer with economies of scale and synergies or a strategic need will place a higher value on the business than a financial buyer seeking profit and cash flow. Each buyer may place a different value, so most exits are handled on an 'offers' basis, enabling the market to decide the value. If the sale has been positioned correctly this enables a number of offers to be secured, and therefore an element of auction to occur to drive the exit value. This requires negotiation skill. A lead advisor will create a buffer to create flexibility, reduce disagreement and manage negotiations to the shareholders' best advantage. Years of experience should help them leverage buyer motivation and spot buyer tactics and combat them effectively. It will also enable them to ensure the right deal terms are structured, particularly as earn-outs – where sums are retained depending on future performance – are now more prevalent in sales.

When choosing a lead advisor it is important to qualify very carefully their connections and research facilities. Who exactly will run the project? What is their success rate per project? Do they have the expertise, experience and ability to align themselves with the shareholder outlook? Ideally, fees will be mainly on success. If M&A is to be part of your journey, the advisor needs to be someone that takes the time to understand your outlook and critically relate to your aspirations. The selection is ultimately on track record and the individual relationship with the advisor. The right advisor will be capable of both signposting the journey and sharing it, as you should both learn from each other. Essentially, choose a competent corporate advisor with soul.

Securing the right advisor and thus the right buyers will normally ensure the shareholders realise maximum value but negotiation also plays a key part. It is important when presenting a business for sale to be in a position where a sale is an option – not a foregone conclusion – and thus a strong alternative strategy and scope to walk away also needs to be in place. This adds to leverage against the buyer. Further, you and the advisor will need to coordinate very carefully and cohesively to manage the negotiations. This usually means taking the time to understand the buyer's needs, maintain firm but non-adversarial points and give small concessions to win the big points. Acquirers will have read the negotiating rule book, so assume they will employ highly strategic negotiation tactics and be prepared – always keeping in mind what you believe is important to them to ensure you exploit the critical pressure points. This requires very careful listening, research and questioning, whilst being realistic and objective about what you are selling and your strengths and weaknesses in that proposition.

A sale is a complex process and ultimately the strategies and terms agreed need to be simple and backed by good quality, well-prepared information. In the end, the role is to work with the buyer to achieve the sale on a collaborative open approach. The leader/navigator plots the journey ahead to ensure the business is properly equipped to deal with the process and sale journey. An ill-prepared sale (or indeed purchase) expedition that fails, usually sets back a business far more than the aborted fees. The management time and distraction is by far the biggest cost. The more prepared you are for the M&A expedition, the easier and faster it will be.

For many leaders and shareholders, a sale exit is also the start of the next big step in the journey, leading to many new directions. With capital wealth, the options are more open. Increasingly today, a sale is a prelude to another venture or the opportunity to business angel or mentor, to share experience, with secure capital and time wealth. Today many leaders after a business sale choose to continue to engage in business in some way, with a view that a hard day's work remains a contributor to happiness. Be open and in flow and the new opportunities arise. Many try to plan too hard 'what next' after a sale, but usually it's such a big change that it is almost impossible to know how you will feel and what opportunities will occur. Some leaders and sellers work closely with the buyers to help them achieve further success and thus a second bite directly from a further shareholder realisation.

What would you do after a sale?

The target of wealth via shareholder value is a critical part of strategic business thinking and should be considered in all aspects of day-to-day decision making and, whether it is ulti - mately a shareholder value exit or sale, should remain part of the journey, not the destination. For this idea we should, as leaders, take the definition of wealth beyond the purely finan - cial; the best employed business strategies create a wealth of relationships, well-being and understanding which is far more important. The money is the reward, enjoying the game is the journey, and when we arrive at that stop-off point we can then be open to and seek new destinations and directions in abund - ance.

Summary

It is part of the leader's role to design and build shareholder value; profit is only half the equation. The target of wealth via shareholder value is a critical part of strategic business thinking and should be considered in all aspects of day-to-day decision making; whether it is ultimately a shareholder value exit, or 'sale' remains part of the journey not the destination.   For this idea, we should as leaders take the definition of wealth beyond the purely financial; the best employed business strategies create a wealth of relationships, well-being and understanding which is far more important. The money is the reward, enjoying the game is the journey and when we arrive at that stop-off point, we can then be open to and seek new destinations and directions in abundance.

Chapter 8
Mapping the way

Introduction

In this chapter, we look at the role of leadership in planning. As the aim of the book is to give you questions for inspiration, I have avoided the temptation to include traditional business plan - ning models, content lists, templates and examples. These details are aimed at management, while the focus on direction and goals is aimed at leadership in order to create motivation, clarity, confidence and energy in navigating the river.

This is a strategy book so we should recommend creating a really detailed route map that is a carefully crafted, highly researched and detailed business plan with lots of specific actions and financials. However, unless you need such a plan for funding purposes, I would strongly caution against such a map because growing a business is usually a journey and not a destination. Almost every company I have visited, or owner I have met, ended often quite successfully in an entirely different place to the one originally planned. This does not mean they had a flawed plan; it's more the fact that markets move, customers change and you often have to make adjustments, regardless of your plans. Too often, plans are about controlling the river, rather than flowing with or influencing the river. Instead, I use the image of mapping the way, identifying each waypoint, each input, and each next step towards the goal

within the context of an overall greater ideal of making a differ -
ence.

Sharing maps

Navigating and mapping out journey waymarks or clear next-
step goals is an incredibly powerful way of achieving
astounding results. I do, however, urge caution on businesses
being too specific about the destination or eventual end game.
Destinations are often highly-ambitious – the problem being
that they are often too far away and their achievement can
seem almost impossible to many in the team. So whilst auda   -
cious and ambitious visions and end games often mark out
leaders, they can actually leave the team behind. Instead, identi -
fying, promoting and tracking waymarks or next-step goals is
what creates the actions, input and motivation for immediate
results as opposed to concentrating on the end game alone.

- *How specific are your next steps?*

- *How clear are you and the team on these, and how are they
  communicated?*

A great example of the benefit of mapping waymarks or step
goals is the now famous story of Joe Simpson as summarised in
his book and the film Touching the Void. In 1986, Joe was one of
two young climbers who attempted to reach the summit of Siula
Grande in Peru – a feat previously attempted but never
achieved. They reach the peak but, as they descend, Joe falls
and breaks his leg. However, they are forced to continue with
Simon Yates – the second climber – letting Joe out on a rope
every 300 metres and then descending to join him. When Joe
falls off an overhang and does not respond to calls, Simon

(rightly under mountaineering survival rules) makes the tough decision to cut the rope and continue back alone. Joe, however, did survive the fall but had passed out. Coming to, he realises that he is stuck in a crevasse with a broken leg, six miles from base camp with a glacier to cover – in mountaineering terms, 'dead'. Joe's ultimate survival is fascinating. Essentially, he knows that his 'destination' is too far and impossible in his condition, but describes how this hopelessness became inspira - tional. He faced a simple choice: die or keep moving. He then describes how, by focusing exclusively on each next step, he survived. By looking immediately ahead and hopping, crawling or dragging his broken body, he eventually made it back to base camp just two hours before Simon and his team were due to leave.

In this we can see that aiming at and achieving visible but next-step waymarks or goals is incredibly motivating and, step by step, little by little, astounding feats of organisation, change and success can be achieved. How does this advice fit with that given in Chapter 4? 'Ahead' is about navigating with an eye to the future and trying to anticipate a general direction and possible destination against future trends. 'Ahead' in business speak is more about the creative vision; about where your ideal end game is. Mapped waymarks need an overall direction to have been communicated, even if the advice is less concerned with the final/actual end game, otherwise the goals or waymarks will not be cohesive and will appear disjointed.

• *What is your principal direction and why?*

In my visits to companies, I have noted how few leaders talk about goals and vision these days. The problem, I think, is that the difference is too little understood and possibly the concept exhausted in the 1980s and 1990s by the consulting community.

However, identifying and driving at step goals is critical to mapping and creating organisational change against an over- arching end game, without becoming too fixated on that vision.

Looking ahead with clear actions

In my talks for business leaders and Chief Executives, I often ask who has a detailed business plan. On a show of hands, it's usually less than half. On discussion, this is often a reflection of their experience that plans don't survive implementation partic- ularly well. One director describes six months of planning and a 50-page plan, only to be beaten by a competitor on their major client renewal because they were not concentrating on the tender but on the plan. It does make sense, therefore, given the nature of quick-moving markets, to avoid the classic business plan with its attention to detail. Nevertheless, some mapping is still required. It is the starting place for researching how to work more intelligently, and communicating what needs to change. This has been recognised since the start of civilisation and the Art of War, written as long ago as 400 BC, reminds us: "How much more certain is defeat if one does not plan at all. From the way planning is done beforehand, we can predict victory or defeat."

From my research and experience, the plans that do work are the ones where leaders are focused on real-time creative research in the market to gain deeper understanding and clarity of what needs to be changed and done. Plans need to identify clear next-step waymarks and actions, as opposed to being persuasive but out-of-date 'textbooks' with beautifully modelled but flawed financial hypotheses. Quick visual plans are focused on action rather than destination and mapped out from the

bottom up, with the team involved and contributing, self-dir -
ected and multi-disciplined towards their achievement. It's
amazing what a team-driven A4 piece of paper, even with care -
fully hand-drawn sketches, can communicate to create align -
ment and to ensure that waymarks and objectives are easily and
effectively communicated. Further, this avoids lots of grief on
PowerPoint, Word and Excel! Who reads a 50-page report with
reams of numbers that only the FD understands? As they say, a
picture can communicate a thousand words.

Plans that 'talk' about results which the team has no ownership
of, or a vision that is too far away, rarely work. Plans that are
actionable with lots of direct change inputs, aimed at a next-
step waymark and crafted alongside the team with good
research, do work.

- *How much time do you spend on mapping and communic -
  ating clear next-step strategy as opposed to crafting out-of-
  date wishful and weighty business plans?*

- *How involved or aligned are your team in mapping and
  achieving the next-step goals?*

Team contributions

As an example, creating a business plan where the team
contribute and do the waymark setting requires communication
of the direction and the reason for the direction. Then, unless
you are working with highly experienced executives, waymark
setting typically requires training and mentoring to help the
team become more multi-disciplined and thus have the ability to
proactively drive change and the evolution themselves, and at
the same time understand why they may need to do this.

Understandably any new skill and approach can be a destabil - ising process; it would therefore be entirely appropriate in the plan to create a specific talent-development programme including how the organisation can ensure that improvement and goal setting is a continuous process (as explained in Chapter 5, Natural Selection). Is it possible to use the very need to establish such a training and mentoring programme as a method to get the team to be more proactive and drive change themselves? For example, share the concept of the need for evolution and do everything to increase skills and develop talent. Ask the team how they learn best, what they feel they need to learn, and to what degree they want to be monitored, sponsored and supported in such a programme. Allow them the space to build the programme but track progress. It will take time and patience but if you never waver (this is important) and continue with the same change message, eventually the idea of team-driven talent development sponsored by the company will be established as a clear team waymark and ultimately achieved as a continuous process and habit embedded in the organisa - tion – a cultural change. It is surprising how little money is spent on talent development, often less than one per cent, yet staff costs and recruitment are typically over 50%. Unless you are always going to hire the top people (expensive), embedding talent development into the business is critical.

- *Are you self-developing top talent and if so, how?*

So mapping is less about a fancy prospectus plan, which is out of date the second you finish it, and far more about setting out with your team clear, simple and achievable waymarks with actionable changes and tracking. In my view and experience, therefore, effectively planning for change and growth is less about defining the overall destination but more about setting a general direction and working democratically with the team –

taking the time to set out and agree goals with strong simple visuals to reinforce clarity, tracking and communication.

There is one other supporting argument to the idea of team-driven, simple, visual and next-step goals planning. This is speed. Perfectly modelled and superbly presented planning tomes swallow up leadership time and create an 'ivory tower syndrome' with an autocratic message. Top-down plans are usually treated sceptically by teams and there remains almost no team ownership to their achievement; worst of all, the time spent crafting them in the boardroom actively prevents the executives having the time to talk to staff, employees and customers to find out where the river is flowing in real time. The time spent on models, lengthy scene-setting and crafting perfect reports could be spent with the team, creating inspiring team-driven mind maps with agreed next-step goals and action.

Ultimately, as financial professionals, we do need to add maths to the equation. A lot of actions sound great on paper, but some good simple maths and basic models around return on invest - ment can save a lot of time and frustration, making sure you can achieve or exceed revenue and cost objectives. Checking the numbers enables you and your team to authenticate the validity of your ideas and create a basic returns and risk check. So mapping should be action and goals-orientated rather than models and theoretical guesswork, reinforcing the aimed-at standards within the business.

There are a myriad of financial model types in the market place but the key to their effective use is that they are simple enough for the leaders and team to understand, refer back to and check. Spreadsheets that can be read on one screen or one sheet only with micro print should be banished and, instead of complexity, more effort made to ensure that all inputs and consequent outputs are well thought out and/or intelligible.

- *How simple and clear are the numbers and do you and your team 'own' them?*

Design and share the map

So, to support each map we need an overall direction and some financials, but more balanced than the traditional definitive business plan usually includes. The map, which can be as simple as that of a mind map showing the goals and action progress steps, is also an excellent tool to create adhesion, coordination and clarity in team alignment. Simple mapped one-page visuals of the waymarks and possible destination are excellent for clarity and enable all to get behind the initiatives under the 'it will seem obvious to them after a while' premise. In other words, the more repetitive your message, in as many forums as possible, the more the change will happen. The clearer and simpler the map, the easier the communication and the more flow that is achieved. For example, my own professional prac - tice has achieved some strong growth initiatives and actions with good success under what we called a series of 'Good to Great' workshops (after Jim Collins' famous business book). The aim was not the groundbreaking breakthrough, but to secure the little team-driven changes that combine over time to make a significant difference. Of course not all our next-step goals worked; some were good, some flawed, but a select few made a fundamental difference and in each waymark it is the 20% of ideas, 'the select few', that are the winners that drive growth. Even the 80% that were neutral or bad were useful or instructive as they enabled us to see what not to do or focus on.

- *How do you display, track, remind, communicate and repeat your targeted waymarks?*

There remains one more aspect of mapping for me in this book, and it's about creating and sustaining motivation – both personal and from the point of team leadership. By setting out and achieving clear waymarks, you create a very powerful and exciting construct that drives evolution and business change. Further, by aligning the team to their achievement and saying thank you when they succeed, you help your team reach their full potential. Teams feel good when they consistently achieve waymarks, are aware of the contribution they make to the predominant direction of the business and have positive, grateful leaders. They therefore create better results – driving the business at the next-step goals and each time creating improvement.

If a waymark fails, was the goal right? Why did it fail? This creates understanding and links back to talent development. Were there enough resources? Is there a need for a reprimand, or was the goal unclear which is your fault? It is your role to be the standard bearer, so be clear and specific about what people did wrong. Be generally positive about the team or person but specific about the failure, then maintain and carefully track improvements next time.

- *How much do you review and reward/reprimand against your goal achievement?*

Summary

In summary, exceptional business success is rarely achieved when trapped in tradition or the results of other people's thinking. It is achieved by fresh perspectives, design and thought leadership supported by well-mapped and clear step goals, enhanced by determination.

Chapter 9
Balance

Introduction

*In Chapter 3, we examined the concept of flow which is about
reducing exertion and creating a more relaxed state by watching
the market's movements more effectively, identifying trends and
influencing the strategy at the right points, with the right effort,
rather than fighting the market as others do. Balance has some
similarities to flow but it is more about creating sustainability for
strategic leadership. Essentially, it is about self-awareness to
enable you to select and adapt the approaches that are working.
I used earlier the analogy of car design improvements, so the
best way to think of balance is the fine tuning of every aspect of
the engine's and vehicle's performance in every area required to
seek absolute efficiency against your goals or ultimate vision.*

Just in case you were worried, this is not a chapter on work/life
balance. This idea is far too simplistic (and too written about) as
many leaders don't differentiate work from fun. Played right,
work is fun and therefore everything is just part of a whole. The
traditional work/life thinking is almost damaging, suggesting
that 'life' is effectively more important than 'work' and the only
area we can enjoy. Either you are at work or you are not, but
how do we make both experiences positive? Today, with 24/7
accessibility and 24/7 client expectations, the concept is even
more flawed. I get some of my best strategy ideas and thoughts
when running. If I have a particularly complex challenge, I

define it, then put the trainers on and 'run' the problem. Is this life or work? Balance is actually about taking the time to be aware on a 'big picture' basis, both personally and strategically, otherwise you end up in a quagmire of detail and the little issues.

One of the inspirations for this book is Herman Hesse's novel Siddhartha. Hesse's story shares the idea that enlightenment is attained through one's experiences and understanding. For me, seeking balance is where we consciously review these aspects and apply changes or fine tuning with the ultimate goal of unconscious simplicity (achieving balance), experiencing fully awake and alive both business and life. Balance will not guar - antee success but it will increase the chances and make life easier.

To seek balance and absolute efficiency we must have no ownership or territorial hang-ups. It's really very simple. Ask yourself, where is the strategy or my approach out of balance and what needs to change and how? Out of balance might be time, money, resource, or style or a combination of all, but spot the wobbles and correct them to seek alignment to the sum of the parts. Some clients have said they don't believe it's possible and that for me is an interesting opinion. I prefer not to worry about whether it is or isn't and simply seek it. I suspect the answer is that balance, congruence and alignment are achieved at different levels of strategy, and that we must seek points at which we can deliberately break the balance to create change. In other words it's about cycles and being aware of cycles.

I have recently been coaching a start-up and the advice to any new entrepreneur must be that now is not the time to seek balance in relationships or in one's social life. In a start-up, more effort must usually go into the business than is really healthy for social relationships. Think of the business as a young child; it needs nurturing very carefully, and with extra attention and time, until it achieves a degree of robustness. In other words, it's perfectly fine on an aware basis in the start-up cycle to choose to be out of balance, as long as you *are* aware and rectify it later.

When we seek balance in the strategy there are a number of key approaches that are essential as business leaders. The first is to remove judgement. Neither judge nor blame the strategy or yourself, just simply see things as they are and make adjustments. If you see things more objectively and simply, it's so much easier to see what to tune and what to change. To do that, we need to detach ourselves from pre-conceptions, expectations and the pre-programmed belief that we have to master a particular activity. When we let go of these things and just accept and enjoy the activities in question, then none of the other things matter.

Self-management

Balance requires awareness of your emotions. It is vital to avoid overexcitement or disappointment as these create attachment, which reduces objectivity. Just enjoy playing the game and moving around, employing different elements of the strategy. Pressure or stress is being shot at in the trenches; business has no real comparison, so what are you worrying or annoyed about? Some days the business game works, some days it doesn't, but aim to make sure the days that work occur more often than the days that don't. Don't presume to manage others until you can manage yourself.

• *How stressed are you? How do you cope with pressure?*

- *How often do you take the time to enjoy the game?*

Change and keep going. Identify where you as a leader struggle or wobble, and seek strategies to remove or reduce the challenge. If you do fall, get up, keep going and do something differently next time.

- *How objective are you about your own approach?*

- *How do you accept feedback and criticism?*

Be patient. If something is taking longer or not quite working, don't falter, don't be put out, and if the change or strategy ultimately doesn't work, it doesn't matter – enjoy the game, not the winning. Patience and time usually achieve more than strength. A patient approach (that does not mean avoiding deadlines) will give you composure and confidence and you are then more likely to win.

- *How positive is your attitude when things take longer than planned?*

- *How realistic are you on deadlines?*

Seek flow. Relax into the approach of leadership not management, let go of pushing too hard or too consciously and, with focus and concentration, allow your experience to do the work. Have you ever played a game or tried to learn something new and tried too hard? Tension, nerves and stress are all counterproductive and can be the result. Sometimes it's best to allow things to happen; no effort, no interference, just watch and listen.

- *Do you try too hard?*

Objectivity

Remain detached, avoid ownership or territorial hang-ups and let go of your ego in order to serve. The need to be seen as intelligent or right stops most people from being successful. We judge others because we judge ourselves but remove judge - ment and be flexible, doing whatever it takes to not take your - self too seriously. Listen.

- *How judgemental are you?*

- *How important is your ego, and where is it holding you back?*

Analyse and review; then decide, act, evaluate and accept. What's working, what's not; what needs changing, what doesn't; what's right, what isn't; what's in balance and flow, what isn't? Make sure you have the right key performance indicators ideally displayed on a simply designed dashboard and quick to evaluate. Seek the truth and absolute alignment with no ownership of what that is and you will get clarity, simplicity and confidence.

- *How can you keep things simpler, how can you seek simpli - city?*

- *How much do you face the truth and how good are you at securing the truth?*

Be present in the now. There are times for looking ahead, and for looking back; indeed we probably spend the vast majority of our time in these areas – what worked, what didn't, what's next. But actually how often do we just spend time in the present? If you do, your mind becomes more open, relaxed, calm and unconcerned; it is less interrupted by irrelevant thoughts and more focused on the actual, the now, and thus it's easier to see what to do. For most business strategists this is very difficult as we have become almost trained to avoid the now as we seek to create the future change; whereas being present, fully present, increases the quality of your awareness enormously. It's like having the most superhuman senses. Turn off the clutter in your mind and just be there. That is watch, listen, observe, feel, and smell in the moment. Can you enjoy wholly and completely the colour, smell, light, noises and movement of a walk through an autumn wood?

- *Do you turn off the clutter?*

- *What is it like in the now, the present, the actual, and what insights does this give you?*

Know yourself. Embrace who you are, not what you are not; play to your strengths and be your natural self. Accept yourself, then concentrate on the tasks in hand. If you deny who you are, you increase stress and make it difficult to focus on the important strategic changes or even happiness; you are also more receptive to feedback without feeling assailed by it. In knowing yourself, it is also important not to over-define your - self against your role. You may be successful, however you define it, but introduce yourself as a person – not a job title.

- *How open are you about the real you?*

- *Do you waste energy managing a persona?*

Acceptance

Know your thoughts. How often do we look at our unconscious drivers, and how all the diverse messages influence us in real time? When you can recognise and accept your true thoughts as they occur, without ownership, you become empowered. For example, you might feel worried but acknowledge this, don't resist or necessarily even act, just acknowledge, and with this comes much greater clarity. Further, there will always be someone with their own agenda exerting their view but again you can just be aware of it, you don't need to react or resist because you know your own mind. Knowing your thoughts arms you with a form of simple clarity in an utterly complex environment.

- *How much do you truly listen to your own mind; are you too busy to notice your own thoughts?*

Relationships. Engage in respectful, noble relationships; challenge people positively; monitor outputs and results, not process and approach. People are human and with respect and understanding of their needs comes motivation. Your ego impacts your interrelationships dramatically but by serving rather than commanding you increase internal openness and efficiency, talent, development and progress. There was one notable bank CEO who used to walk the shop floor but couldn't be bothered to remember the names of the key players and expected each branch to be painted before the visits – talk about ivory tower syndrome! Balance requires leadership humility, you are not better than others. You may have worked harder, been schooled better or even been luckier – but what does better mean? Balance requires a healthy respect for all contributors and relationship interactions.

Belief and communication. Once you have armed yourself with a more patient, objective and aware approach without ego, your confidence, self-belief and communication skills will build to new levels. You become more in tune with who you are simply with the increased confidence that things will work themselves out.

- *How simple and clear do you keep things?*

- *How humbly confident are you?*

Balance is often urged in life coaching but this rarely gets to the heart of what it really means. It is more about striving for or, even better, being in equilibrium and creating a concept or tool that enables you to make the adjustments needed to ensure that. I have talked here about seeking leadership balance but it can be greater than that. In organisations, for example, seeking change with equilibrium is far more effective than seeking stability, which can lead to managing the status quo. Ensuring values are balanced can in itself be powerful. In today's world of 24/7, do you really care if your team are in or out the office or surfing in work time? More importantly, what do the team achieve, against what goals and targets, and how are these monitored? The world changes – so it is better to deal with it and recognise that staff respond better to freedom designed in the right way.

Many people, as I have suggested above, too often see balance as seeking the right time split between work and life. This is relevant, but I hope you can see that I am seeking to use the concept in a 'total picture' way to give you visualisation or cent-ralisation to tune and create constant adjustment. Received wisdom is that time management is important, but is it really possible? You can't manage time; the clock ticks whether you seek to beat it, manage it or even shout at it, although I am sure you have tried this! Instead, in balance, we must seek pace, effi-ciency, presence and clarity of use in the time available to us. We must be wholly aware of when we are being wasteful, whether it is in the quality of the story you read your child at night or the improved effectiveness (time or result) of your board meetings because you have prepared more.

- *How wasteful are you?*

Every moment is spent choosing what we do and don't do and seeking effectiveness, fulfilment, results and pleasure and the balance concept creates the adjustment mechanism. Balance is personal and the outlook shifts with your age and the zeitgeist – the spirit of the age or current intellectual and social fashion. Circumstances change and ambitions change. As an example, the whole retirement concept amuses me. The Victorians and previous ages never had it, and it was largely invented by the Western world's pensions industry in the 1950s. But with such improvements in life expectancy, the idea has virtually become redundant, yet why are we finding it so difficult to accept this change? My current outlook is wind down but continue to dabble, keep active and involved. What is your 'retirement' outlook? Balance requires objectivity, self-awareness and the ability to look forward, to dance to the tune of the times or change calmly rather than tensely fighting; if you fight you usually fragment or at best tire yourself out.

- *How aware of the zeitgeist are you?*

Balance is about aligning yourself and your strategy to the things you love and the passions you have in a strategic way that is right for the business; managing and tuning, to engage the equal pressures of these aspects and their different needs, to create equilibrium. It's about seeking to learn new things, doing things differently and enjoying it; accepting that some ideas will work and some will fail, whilst staying fit and helping others to work, play, design, tune and enjoy.

In Chapter 2, we discussed that an objective understanding of your preferences, time focus and habits is critical to creating changes in both you and your organisation. I hope you will see a large part of balance comes from adjusting the outlook and thus the output but, as with any new skill, achieving balance requires patience. There has been much work and study on the idea that talent is a myth and that most exceptional success comes from practice, the right mentors and the environment. Of course, some leaders come more armed with balance and whether this is nature or nurture we choose not to debate. The most positive belief is that your habits form your results and that these can gradually be altered with patience and practice.

When you first learn a new language your efforts are clumsy, but there are many people who achieve competence via practice and immersion; many even achieve the higher state of being able to think in a language. The metaphor is that our brains form our habits and they do this in language so you can create and adopt a new 'mental language' and thus sustain new habits, outlooks and better balance. If you choose to share your changes and thoughts on outlook be aware that, for some, this can be equally as daunting as learning a new language so they will need support in the transition. Patience will be required whilst you translate.

New habits and balance take time and initially it feels uncom   - fortable, but practice can and does make it unconscious. It might take you a hundred times on one thought angle to get there but don't give up. It is through practice that we learn and with the experience and wisdom gained we can create new perspectives and build a broader vision.

- *When did you last question your habits?*

- *How much does your brain take the 'old' easy route – even though deep down you know it doesn't work?*

Seeking a positive outlook

Why have I opted for balance as an idea rather than, say, the more traditional strategic MBA theories of continual change such as the well-known Japanese Kaizen theories of improve - ment? These theories are excellent and worth a mention but they focus on tuning the 'hard or tangible' strategy such as process, design ideas or performance enhancements. They tend to ignore the alignment between the leadership and the strategy. Normally, in any business, what the leaders are good at works well and what they are bad at does not work well; but, by seeking balance, leaders can individually make adjustments to their outlook, as well as looking at the values, goals and ethos in the business. Seeking balance, therefore, is more compre - hensive and is about achieving breakthroughs in both the tangible strategies and the soft or intangible personal strategies. Fundamentally, balance is about putting the ego and the politics aside and taking a long, hard look at the organisa - tion and yourself as leader and then making adjustments as necessary. There is no territory, there is no turning aside, no denial, no blame, just the drive for absolute excellence with all aspects converging to achieve improvement.

- *Which of your current habits are good or bad?*

- *What beliefs do you need to challenge?*

- *Are your current responsibilities the right ones?*

- *How much do you control your responsibilities and time as opposed to the business?*

- *What do you need, as opposed to want, to put time and energy into?*

- *Are you a bottleneck with too many people seeking the solutions from you?*

- *How aware of the fine tuning elements are you?*

- *How distracted are you?*

Balance, in this context, is about not agonising over the niggling details such as does that person like me, or are they good at their job? Will we win the contract, or why do I get annoyed when...? Yes, we are aware of these questions, but what *really* matters? Balance is more about seeking a truly objective 'big picture' view by turning off the filter and accepting the truth. Beyond the ego and the politics, what is the deep truth that we can see? Once we see the truth we can make the real adjustments that win. Seeking an objective under - standing of what's real and true right now makes life more rewarding and drives both personal fulfilment, purposefulness, business growth and shareholder value.

Summary

In the idea of seeking balance, we have a continual quest to seek absolute congruence or alignment, constantly tuning to achieve this in an aware way. Imagine your mind and business strategy as a river. You are aware there are diversions, falls, rocks, white water, eddies, currents and flows formed by the market, ideas, strategies and emotions. Each can potentially create a different diversion or course, some good and some bad; thus the river's course itself can either flow simply and clearly, or it can become disrupted because there is no indi - vidual, leadership or organisational awareness and acceptance of what needs to change or how to achieve balance. These diversions in the river create pain, suffering, void and stress. In balance, we train ourselves for control and total awareness to make the right adjustments at the right time to avoid diversions and to navigate the right course. Thus we allow all the aspects to move together, creating growth and sustainability in the river, your leadership and the strategy.

Chapter 10
Journey or destination

Introduction

The whole is greater than the sum of its parts, so in this chapter my focus is to interlink many of the concepts I have set out, but with a fundamental aspiration in their connection. I would like to shift, if I can, the achievement focus that most leaders seem to have in spades to a more humble enjoyment of the adventure focus; to move the main objective, that usually exists, from measuring and counting the result – 'the destination' – to an outlook of actually enjoying the adventure in seeking the result – simply put, enjoying 'the journey'.

I have set out the idea that business leaders and owners have a responsibility to move strategically from management to leadership by spending more time on business design, research, new products, alliances and acquisitions rather than management and organisation. By delegating more effectively, 'management' time can then be spent in the strategy space to drive sustainable growth and also work more effectively on shareholder value and market competitiveness. Simultaneously this can combine with a change of personal outlook to reduce stress, and increase ease. To help I have examined some of the possible personal barriers and asked key questions that I hope might help to set out a proven personal journey; the need to listen more, put aside the ego and find the truth more passively and confidently.

I typically meet and visit in my role as a professional advisor more than one hundred companies a year, small to corporate. The good companies that achieve growth, even in difficult markets, seem to me to always share the same common denominator – that is, leaders who have taken the time with their teams to research and then create a clear and confident strategy with specific actions. They then engage their key reports and team with simple accountability and appropriate support to deliver the plan whilst listening carefully to what is working and what isn't. Of course everyone has different resources or skills in this approach, and not all have a secure enough base for being strategic, but it surprises me just how many companies who do have the resource nevertheless do not engage strategically. As we examined in Chapter 8, this goes beyond business planning. It's about the leader's absolute clarity in where they should be focused, simplicity of the step goals, and why they are important. Leaders have the responsibility to look at what they do well and what they don't, and consider what changes they should make in their own outlook and personal journey. For many it is risk and uncertainty that holds them back, for some it's overcomplicating and being distracted, and for others it's too many ideas.

My own personal experience here may be useful. I am hardworking in combination with being proud, imaginative and impatient. We enjoyed business success young but we plateaued and we could not work out why. We employed the usual strategy – push harder, faster – and (surprise!) we continued to plateau, yet the same strategy had delivered in some years over 40% growth which was pretty exceptional in professional practices. Why did we plateau? We could blame more competition or the market but…we only have to look at old school reports, Myers-Briggs analysis, and work appraisals; it's all there. Being a hard worker meant I felt guilty not being at the front driving the whole time (making the business overdependent on me). It also made me a poor delegator. Being impatient meant that I struggled to take the time to research properly, let things play out or bring attention to detail. My overactive creativity left us with too many options and initiatives, none being done well, and an unclear team. Finally, my pride meant that even when the hints were there, I was not listening. Of course I have many strengths too and being hardworking with endurance and imagination gave me the power to create something from nothing. My point is that, actually, the key to creating leap shifts in growth is often as much about leadership self-awareness as it is about strategy. It's not about what you are or are not, it is about being aware of where you are and your personal saboteurs and then being more flexible in your outlook.

- *How are your strengths and weaknesses helping or hindering you at this stage of your journey?*

In writing this book, my aim has not been to provide a definitive expert guide on all business aspects and strategy, but more to provide an insight into growing businesses for personal satisfaction whilst aiming at making a bigger, more purposeful contribution to society and wealth generation. I have sought with my questions to navigate a broader perspective on business and a personal approach to, I hope, help you examine more objectively and review what's good and bad in what you and your team do. I have also tried to balance the trusted 'hard' logic aspects of business strategy; that is, the strategic ideas, such as evolution, and better key performance indicators or dashboard, along with challenges in how you spend your time and your personal outlook.

If you recall, one of my initial inspirations for the river in this title was from the idea that it is the richness of one's experiences and journey that creates understanding and from that comes fulfilment. Few of us know why we are here on Earth and the more science makes us agnostic, the less purpose we have on the surface of it, which many find increasingly dissatisfying and many have dangerously lost their moral compass. For example, global banking by 2008 had a culture of greed resulting in a near global financial meltdown due to poor basic decisions. This is because, as agnosticism grows, no one today is effectively setting our values, and we are therefore in danger of defining and measuring success purely and dissatisfyingly on just the accumulation of wealth, fame and power – forgetting relationships, social harmony and purposefulness in doing the 'right' thing by others. However, if we stop and reflect, the more truly exciting the times we live in are, whether you are religious or not, humans are more and more defining their own values and working together. We are, for the first time on a global scale, cooperating and sharing knowledge, ideas and technology – resulting, in the last 60 years, in less death through war, less famine and disease, and more opportunity and education. Yes, there are still big problems but, overall, the progress and opportunity in globally leading more meaningful, ethical and cooperative lives has been extraordinary and, further, we have achieved this despite a hugely increasing population.

The 2008 financial crash was averted due to global government and company interaction, coordination and accord. Today, climate change is our biggest threat but will we achieve the same coordinated counter response? A little late perhaps, but that's human nature. Today we communicate globally for better human rights, more freedom, more connection, more stability and more wealth, and I believe we each have an individual responsibility to work together to do our personal best, to do what is right by others, and to define our opportunity and contribution in that progress.

- *What can you do to contribute more as you make your way towards your destination?*

The destination is not just the number of new cars you can buy as you accumulate, but the way you get there is just as important; if you like, the journey is in itself the destination. For example, what is the point in 15-hour days behind the desk in order to buy a high-end, two-seater sports car which depreciates like a stone and which you can't even enjoy with your kids? Why not work fewer hours and spend more time with the kids and say no to the marketing man who created the need for the car to flatter your ego? Of course this is an opinion, but I am suggesting that we might just try to be more aware of our decision making and seek balance in our choices. I am not saying don't be a capitalist, just be more aware of your choices and how it impacts on your time, stress and ability to have inner satisfaction through a better journey. This is about redefining wealth to its more traditional definition, one that combines a journey of achieving wisdom, experiences and relationships as well as capital, income and self-actualisation.

The Dalai Lama in his book *The Pursuit of Happiness* sets out that in the Western world he knows more unhappy people than in the East. This is because the Western quest seems to be for the most toys, trophies and money. The dichotomy however is that the more you have, the more it owns you and you end up running around looking after it rather than focusing on your business and relationship wealth. The business people I see succeed have no shortage of fine material possessions, but they always try to keep it in balance with what they can actually afford and properly use, and is low stress to own and organise. They choose their own journey rather than worry about the marketing man's or society's expectations of what they should and shouldn't do or have. They embrace simplicity in the pursuit of focus, optimum energy levels and self-defining their contribution and journey. I have used the word 'journey' but a better word might be 'adventure' as this creates a picture of the hidden treasure, movement, excitement and energy of life's journey. There are, of course, risks in adventures which need to be managed, but adventures are rich in experience and discovery and there are as many adventures as there are questions you can think of to ask.

All sequences can be thought of as a journey, from the process of a customer buying your products to the course of one's life. Implied however, is that journeys are intentional, with a route planned in advance, with a defined starting point and destination. Of course, the same applies with business plans, and I am urging in the above that we avoid the prevalent quick-wins thinking and temporary destinations and instead find a route that is more enjoyable and sustainable long term. I don't suggest you neglect earning money, far from it, but I do suggest that you place its pursuit further down the agenda; for example, many truly great strategic initiatives take 24 months or more to even gain traction, let alone bear fruit. Are you and your shareholders this patient and prepared for a broader horizon?

- *What is your direction?*

All planned journeys break down into stages from one waymark to the next. These steps should focus on the inputs as opposed to the outputs; that is, the specific actions required not the results desired. For example, if you berate the sales team for not hitting their targets – fine, but if you or the Sales Director don't monitor how many calls the team need to make and look at increasing conversion rates to hit those targets, your berating simply becomes a rant. I appreciate that if you are experienced, this inputs/outputs idea is basic, but how often do organisations set the wrong outputs and give no direction on inputs? Further, the outputs must align with customer expectations, both internally and externally. As an example, I pay for 'private' banking but I still have to do the security checks, ID work and call waiting when I want to change or update something and, further, I have a different team from the bank to the credit card team. Call me romantic, but my idea of 'private' is where I am important and people make things happen around me, not where I have to go into a call waiting position. The banking service I actually pay for is quite reasonable and gives some nice benefits in insurance, but I just hate the description 'private' as this conjures up so much more than the service actually delivers. Effectively, the name of the service is not aligned to the customer's hope, and the inputs need to be more carefully described to match the end goal and expectation.

'Journey' is a tried and tested business metaphor for setting the direction well and, against that, the interim step-goals or inputs. Too often, however, the focus is destination, usually defined as 'we need more results and pressure with no changes or support!' Instead, how can you design and lead a team and market-driven business with clearer success steps so you enjoy the journey better? How can you run a business where you can 'dream' and look for the strategy and ideas that make a real difference; seeking fulfilment in the process and the journey, not the destination?

As leaders, it is paramount that we set the standards for the plans, both the interim steps and the outlook, but I do believe that it needs to be a journey with the ambition of a rewarding, enjoyable approach. When was the last time you and your board actually had a real business belly laugh? I am not saying don't take business seriously, but take a little more time to enjoy it, set clearer and simpler interim steps and it can then yield amazing fruit. A senior team with patience, a sense of humour, understanding, creativity and interim focus is far more dynamic than an overdriven, financially uptight team. Ambitious and driven can still apply – indeed they are fundamental – but with a polite smile and sportsmanship. A journey where the focus is enjoyment can be designed whatever the activity but it takes effort, imagination and steady continuous investment in its importance. Furthermore, the single biggest retention driver is friendships at work, so focusing on enjoyment is actually cost effective. Enjoyment contributes to success rather than undermines it, as long as you make sure the interim steps are clear and measurable. Some of the most successful teams appear from the outside to be the most laissez-faire and seem to succeed effortlessly, but actually this is often about celebrating the carefully designed and orchestrated approach and process built at the outset.

- *How well do you define enjoyment, accountability and standards?*

Leaders that put themselves and their ego aside to gain better understanding in the pursuit of excellence tend to succeed more. I suspect this is because they are more objective about what is and isn't working in both their outlook and their businesses. For good case studies in this, please refer to the research carried out by Jim Collins in his popular book *Good to Great* (2001). The research, from 143 companies sampled, showed that those with exceptional growth all had a common thread: leaders with humility, seeking success for their team and organisations – not just for their own personal financial success. A key element of this objectivity comes from just watching, creating, listening and being mindful, that is positively alert. Quality systems, technical knowledge, finances, brand and skills all have a bearing of course; indeed, I have argued strongly for this in the book. Ultimately, however, it is the objective clarity, focus and state of mind of the team and the leadership that drives growth and shareholder value. Too often we let our lives be built by history or habit and we allow constant access, demand and contact to remove our space for objectivity, our ability to think, listen and understand the journey. Leaders who make that space, drive growth and shareholder value as a result. One Mr Bill Gates, I am told, still takes a 'think week' every year where he does nothing but read, research and contemplate.

- *How humble, simple and focused are you?*

In business leadership communication, it is through abstract stories and metaphors that we usually – and perhaps ironically – achieve better clarity, understanding and team awareness. In this story, the river is the market and it ebbs and flows. All rivers ultimately reach the ocean only to then evaporate and turn to rain. The river is therefore continuous and interconnected without beginning or end, and thus it is with global markets and businesses. If we recognise this interconnection and continuity, and take the time to study the ebbs and flows, unity and opportunity can be spotted and understanding progressed as well as a deeper purpose achieved. Additionally, in the river metaphor, we see that leaders can only go forward as a river can never flow backwards. Consequently, we can see that strategic decisions cannot be undone and that past decisions create ripples of change that cannot be stopped. In this respect, we must flow onwards – recognising this constant forward and ahead movement, embracing the evolution and historic ripples, navigating and mapping more effective courses and waymarks.

- *Are you learning faster than the world is changing?*

Summary

I believe that you have the resources, in whatever sector, to create a more sustainable business with better shareholder value. There are few 'grand inventions' or 'big ideas' that will drive these changes – it's more about the leadership's focus and outlook in researching, setting the direction clearly and creating a designed environment of team-driven rapid change. You may be an experienced navigator/traveller in the business river or a new one, but are you learning faster than the world is changing? Inspiration, learning, positive fulfilment, flow, success and confidence are a state of mind. How are you writing your story?

Inspirations and thanks

Firstly I dedicate the book to my readers; thank you. Then to friends and family for their amazing support; love you. Then to my editors for correcting my meanderings; amazing. I also dedicate the book to a select few mentors (you know who you are) that have held the mirror up time and time again to keep me intact, and finally to my clients for allowing me to serve and gain over 20 years' experience of seeing which are the more successful strategies and outlooks to adopt in business leader - ship.

A thank you note to some business greats...

In Search of Excellence, **Tom Peters** . For the idea that successful companies know and recruit to their culture, get close to their customers, stay management lean and have a bias for action – 'getting on with it'.

E-Myths, **Michael E Gerber**. For the idea that most businesses fail because the founders are technicians who were inspired to start a business without knowledge of how successful busi - nesses run. To work on rather than in a business is the key to success so that leaders are freed from most daily operations to spend more time on strategic issues.

The Power of Servant Leadership, **Robert Greenleaf**. For the idea that better leadership is avoiding the status or power-driven leader but instead sharing power, putting the needs of others first, and helping people develop and perform as highly as possible.

Good to Great, **Jim Collins** . For the idea, secured via careful study, that great companies are built from good – usually by internal leaders with long service and expertise who are humble, but driven to serve, and do what's best for the company. First 'who', then 'what': get the right people on the bus, then figure out where to go. Find the right people and try them out in different positions.

The 22 Immutable Laws of Marketing, **Al Ries and Jack Trout**. For the idea that products are about perception, not reality, and that we can design this perception. If the universe exists, it exists inside your own mind and the minds of others. That's the reality that marketing programmes and business leaders must deal with.

***Bounce – The Myth of Talent and the Power of Practice,*
Matthew Syed**. For the idea that 10,000 hours' practice in the
right environment and with the right coaches will usually result
in extraordinary talent.